DATE DUE

The Power of One

The Power of One

Daisy Bates and the Little Rock Nine

by Judith Bloom Fradin & Dennis Brindell Fradin

Clarion Books • New York

Clarion Books
a Houghton Mifflin Company imprint
215 Park Avenue South, New York, NY 10003
Copyright © 2004 by Judith Bloom Fradin and Dennis Brindell Fradin

The text was set in 11-point Centennial 55 Roman.

www.houghtonmifflinbooks.com

Printed in the U.S.A.

Library of Congress Cataloging-in-Publication Data

Fradin, Judith Bloom.
The power of one : Daisy Bates and the Little Rock Nine / by Judith Bloom Fradin and
Dennis Brindell Fradin.
p. cm.
Includes bibliographical references and index.
ISBN 0-618-31556-X
1. Bates, Daisy—Juvenile literature. 2. African American women civil rights workers—Arkansas—
Little Rock—Biography—Juvenile literature. 3. Civil rights workers—Arkansas—Little Rock—
Biography—Juvenile literature. 4. School integration—Arkansas—Little Rock—History—20th
century—Juvenile literature. 5. Central High School (Little Rock, Ark.)—Juvenile literature.
6. Little Rock (Ark.)—Race relations—Juvenile literature. I. Fradin, Dennis B. II. Title.
F419.L7F73 2004
323'.092—dc22   2004004618

ISBN-13: 978-0-618-31556-7
ISBN-10: 0-618-31556-X

MP 10 9 8 7 6 5 4 3 2 1

For Fran Dyra, who made it all happen

For their many hours of gracious assistance,
the authors would like to thank the following people:

In Huttig, Arkansas:

Louis Boyette	Distant relative of Daisy Bates
Clifton Broughton	Daisy Bates's adoptive cousin
Laura Manning	A resident of Huttig
Jovon Smith	Distant relative of Daisy Bates

In Little Rock, Arkansas:

Jan Brown	Daisy Bates's goddaughter
Elizabeth Eckford	One of the Little Rock Nine
Reverend Leroy James	Friend and helper in Mrs. Bates's later years
Vearlon Jeffries	The Bateses' across-the-street neighbor
Aaron Lovelace	Ms. Jeffries's nephew; Daisy Bates used to baby-sit for him
Laura A. Miller	Chief of interpretation and cultural resources, Central High School National Historic Site, Little Rock
Courtney Peeples	Ms. Jeffries's son; delivered *State Press* for Mrs. Bates
David Ware	Capitol Historian, Arkansas Secretary of State's Office

In the Chicago area:

Beatrice Cowser Epps	Daisy Lee's childhood friend
David E. Neely	Lottie Neely's son, cousin to L.C. Bates
Lottie Brown Neely	L.C. Bates's first cousin
Thelma Mothershed Wair	One of the Little Rock Nine

Contents

Daisy Bates.

Introduction

"The Bravest Woman I Have Ever Known"

Daisy Bates was one of the great civil rights leaders of the twentieth century. For many years she and her husband, L.C. Bates, published the *Arkansas State Press,* an influential black newspaper. Mrs. Bates also served as president of the Arkansas branch of the National Association for the Advancement of Colored People (NAACP), participated in federal anti-poverty programs, and wrote an award-winning autobiography. But she is best remembered for her work during the Little Rock school crisis of 1957–58.

In 1954 the United States Supreme Court ruled that segregating students by race in public schools must end. Many southern cities resisted the high court's order to integrate schools. When nine black students entered Central High School in Little Rock, Arkansas, thousands of white people protested. As her state's NAACP president, Daisy Bates guided those black students, known as the Little Rock Nine, through a school year filled with physical and verbal abuse. Mrs. Bates herself became a target of racists, who shattered her windows, burned crosses on her lawn, and waged a campaign to destroy her newspaper. To make things more difficult, the Arkansas governor did all he could to keep Little Rock's schools segregated. As the mentor of the Little Rock Nine, Mrs. Bates helped establish school integration in the South.

She was called "the beautiful and indomitable Daisy Bates" by Will Campbell, a preacher who helped her at a crucial point in the struggle. Comparing her to a great black leader who had fought slavery, Reverend Campbell added: "Not since Sojourner Truth has there been such a woman. Mrs. Bates, as head of the NAACP, nurtured and suffered with the children through it all."

She stood up to the bigots so resolutely that the assistant principal of Central High School, Elizabeth Huckaby, wrote: "The devil himself could not have been more abhorred by the segregationists than Daisy Bates."

"Daisy Bates is the bravest woman I have ever known," wrote Adolphine Fletcher Terry, who also stepped forward to help. "When the [nine] black children started at Central High, every day the students came to her house after school. They would discuss the day they had had and she would encourage and tell them what they were doing for their race. Rocks were thrown at her house and the windows were broken many times. She was given no protection by the police, but she never wavered and certainly never gave up."

Mrs. Bates worked for civil rights into her old age. Although the racists put the *State Press* out of business, she dreamed of reviving the newspaper. She did so in 1984, at the age of seventy.

Perhaps the most remarkable aspect of Daisy Bates was that she achieved all this despite a difficult start in life. Born in a small town in rural Arkansas, she was left alone in the world as a small child when her mother was murdered and her father fled to escape the same fate. Fortunately, family friends adopted her. The love and attention they gave the parentless child helped her become the dedicated civil rights leader Daisy Bates.

Judith Bloom Fradin
Dennis Brindell Fradin

The Power of One

Daisy and L.C. Bates's house.

1

"THE NEXT WILL BE DYNAMITE"

Daisy Bates expected trouble in the late summer of 1957, only she thought it would come after Labor Day, when school opened.

Mrs. Bates lived in Little Rock, the capital of Arkansas, where she was state president of the National Association for the Advancement of Colored People. In that capacity she was closely involved in a landmark event that was scheduled to occur in early September. As in other southern states, Arkansas cities and towns were strictly segregated. Black people were excluded from, or limited to inferior facilities in, schools, hospitals, libraries, parks, buses, and restrooms.

In response to a U.S. Supreme Court decision, Little Rock was supposed to start integrating its schools on Tuesday, September 3, 1957. A small group of black students was to enter the city's previously all-white Central High School on that day. Having fought for school integration for many years, Arkansas NAACP president Daisy Bates was now becoming the black students' chief mentor and spokesperson.

She knew that integrating Central High wouldn't be easy. White people who insisted on maintaining segregated schools were forming committees, some of which vowed to block the entry of the black students by any means possible. But not until the evening of August 22 did Daisy Bates fully realize how dangerous the segregationists could be.

1

On that Thursday night, Mrs. Bates watched the eleven-P.M. news on her living room TV. The news was disturbing. That evening a local segregationist group called the Capital Citizens' Council had hosted a dinner at Little Rock's Hotel Marion. They had brought in Georgia's governor, Marvin Griffin, as the featured speaker. Some 350 people had paid $10 (the equivalent of about $70 in today's money) apiece to hear Governor Griffin denounce the Supreme Court's school integration order. Forcing previously all-white schools to admit black students was an attack on the South's "way of life" and an attempt "by force to destroy our government," Governor Griffin told the cheering audience. He urged white southerners to resist integration and called the Capital Citizens' Council a "courageous group of Arkansas patriots who are fighting a dedicated battle to preserve the rights of states."

What a perversion of the word "patriot," thought Daisy Bates as she watched the broadcast. "Patriot" was usually applied to people like George Washington, Nathan Hale, and Benjamin Franklin. How could a group of white people who wanted to exclude black teenagers from an all-white high school be called "patriots"? But the most harmful aspect of the Capital Citizens' Council gathering was the effect it could have on the Arkansas governor, Orval Faubus.

Up to that point it hadn't been clear whether Governor Faubus would go along with the school integration plan or oppose it. Griffin's rousing reception made it more likely that Faubus would cave in to the segregationists and try to keep the black students out of Central High. Faubus and Griffin certainly appeared to be in agreement. Griffin was staying at Faubus's guest house, and the two governors were having breakfast together the next morning.

Following the news broadcast, Mrs. Bates switched off the TV and took Skippy, the family cocker spaniel, out for his final walk of the day. Upon returning home, Mrs. Bates sat down on the living room couch by the picture window and began leafing through a newspaper. She and her husband, Lucius Christopher Bates, known to everyone as L.C., were the publishers of the *Arkansas State Press,* one of the South's leading black-oriented weekly newspapers. She liked to compare the *Press*'s reporting style to that of Little Rock's leading white papers, the *Arkansas Gazette* and the *Arkansas Democrat.*

Daisy Bates was glancing through a newspaper when suddenly she heard what sounded like an explosion. The forty-three-year-old civil rights leader and newspaper publisher instinctively hit the floor and covered her head. L.C. ran into the room and found his wife lying on the floor.

"Are you hurt? Are you hurt?" L.C. asked.

Although covered with glass and bleeding slightly from numerous small cuts, Daisy was otherwise unharmed. "I don't think so," she answered. Rising to her feet, she picked up the rock that had burst through the picture window. A note was attached to the rock by a string. Unfolding the paper, Mrs. Bates read the note and then showed it to her husband:

THE NEXT WILL BE DYNAMITE
K.K.K.

"A message from the Arkansas *patriots*," said Daisy Bates, sarcastically mocking the Georgia governor's speech. She and L.C. knew that "K.K.K." stood for Ku Klux Klan, a white racist hate group known for violence against black people.

"Thank God their aim was poor," said L.C. He called the police, but they had little interest in trying to find out who had thrown the rock.

The couple patched up the window with masking tape, then went to bed, but Daisy couldn't sleep. She kept reliving the moment the rock had hit the window, when she had thought the house was being bombed. All through the night questions raced through her mind.

Might some racist actually dynamite their home? What would the bigots do to the black students when they tried to enter Central High in less than two weeks? What would Governor Faubus do? Would the segregationists try to destroy the newspaper that had provided a living for L.C. and Daisy Bates for the past sixteen years?

In her autobiography, *The Long Shadow of Little Rock,* Daisy Bates later recalled her troubled state of mind that night:

This rock and accompanying note crashed through the Bateses' window.

As State President of the National Association for the Advancement of Colored People I was in the front-line trenches. Was I ready for war? Was I ready to risk everything that L.C. and I had built? Who was I really and what did I stand for? Toward dawn I knew I had found the answer.

Daisy Bates finally drifted off to sleep, no longer plagued by doubt or uncertainty.

Woods near Huttig, Arkansas, photographed around the time of Daisy Lee's birth.

2

"Niggers Have to Wait"

Some important facts about Daisy Bates's birth are not known.

We know that she was born Daisy Lee Gatson in Huttig, a small sawmill town in far southern Arkansas near the Louisiana border. We know that her mother was a black woman named Millie Riley Gatson. But neither her exact date of birth nor her father's identity is known with certainty.

Various sources list the year of her birth as 1912, 1914, 1920, and 1922. The problem is, no original birth certificate exists for Daisy Lee Gatson. Many southern towns kept scanty records for black people in the early 1900s. Black children frequently were born at home, and no one bothered to make or place on file official records of their birth. In a 1957 interview L.C. Bates told a newspaper reporter that his wife had been born thirty-five years earlier, "give or take a couple years," which would make her birth year sometime between about 1920 and 1924.

A more reliable source on the subject would seem to be a "delayed birth certificate" that Daisy Lee Gatson Bates filed for herself with the Arkansas Bureau of Vital Statistics in 1962. She listed November 11, 1914, as her date of birth on this document. But that date appears to be wrong too. Daisy Bates's closest childhood friend was Beatrice Cowser, now Beatrice Cowser Epps, whom we interviewed a few days before her ninetieth birthday.

"That's not right," Mrs. Epps says about the 1914 date her friend Daisy gave on the delayed birth certificate. "I was born on February 28, 1913, and Daisy was born the same year, sometime between September and November. We started school on the same day and were always in the same grade." So the most likely date for Daisy Lee Gatson's birth—according to her best childhood friend—is sometime between September and November of 1913.

On her delayed birth certificate Daisy Bates listed her father as John Gatson. But that is in doubt too. A niece of Daisy's who did some research concluded that a relative of John Gatson's named Hezekiah Gatson was actually her father.

Sadly, Daisy Lee Gatson never knew her real parents. One of the least-talked-about aspects of life in the South was the fact that many black women were raped by white men who never faced any legal consequences. When Daisy Lee was a very young child, her mother was raped and murdered. Ninety years later, several people who knew the story told us what happened.

"Daisy Lee's mother was a pretty lady, and the fellows liked her very much," said Mrs. Epps. "Before she got married, she had a white sweetheart. But then she married and had a baby, Daisy Lee, in 1913. Her former sweetheart wanted to continue the relationship, but she now had a husband and baby and refused." Late one night Daisy Lee's mother was lured away from home by a false message that her husband had been injured on his job at the sawmill. Millie Gatson asked a neighbor to watch her baby and rushed off toward the mill to see about her husband.

She never arrived. Someone who was lying in wait raped and killed Millie Gatson, then left her body at the edge of the town's Forty Acre Pond. It was rumored that her former sweetheart had murdered her.

While in Huttig we met Daisy's cousin Clifton Broughton. Mr. Broughton showed us the spot along Forty Acre Pond where Millie Riley Gatson's lifeless body was found. He told us more about the murder.

At least two white men were involved in killing Daisy's mother, said Mr. Broughton. A black man in town knew who they were and told authorities, but nothing was ever done. In fact, the black man who had identified the murderers was himself in danger of being killed, so he fled Huttig in an unusual way. "He was smuggled out of town in a casket," said Mr. Broughton. "He never came back as far as I know." The man who escaped Huttig hiding in a casket may have been Daisy's father, who fled town after his wife's murder to get beyond the killers' reach. But before he departed, her father placed Daisy with friends in Huttig named Orlee and Susie Smith. This childless couple adopted Daisy and didn't tell her about her biological parents until she was eight years old.

Located in a big lumbering region, Huttig had grown up around the Union Saw Mill, the town's main business. Most of the 1,250 people who lived in Huttig worked for the mill, whose owners basically ran the town. The sawmill owned many of the homes in Huttig, and most of the townspeople purchased their food and other supplies at the sawmill "commissary." Besides this general store, Huttig's small business district included the meat market, post office, movie theater, and ice cream parlor.

Like other southern cities and towns, Huttig was racially segregated. Forty Acre Pond, near the center of town, separated the races. On one side of the pond was White Town, which Daisy Bates later recalled as a place of "white bungalows, white steepled churches, a white spacious school with a big lawn," and of course white people. On the other side of the pond was Negro Town. Many residents of this black neighborhood lived in "shotgun cottages"—little homes in which the rooms were arranged in a straight line. To brighten up their neighborhood, the people of Negro Town painted their cottages and two churches red.

Huttig's ice cream parlor, 1907.

A shotgun cottage.

While Huttig's white children attended their spacious school, the black children went to "a two-room schoolhouse equipped with a potbellied stove that never quite succeeded in keeping it warm," Daisy Bates later remembered. In the winter Daisy Lee, Beatrice Cowser, and their classmates had to sit in school all day wearing their coats. A lack of books was another chronic problem. The black students learned to read from old hand-me-down books donated by the white school. "I remember our first reader, *Bow-Wow-Wow, Whose Dog Art Thou?*" said Mrs. Epps. "There were between sixty and seventy students in our school, with three teachers for all eight grades."

Only later did Daisy Lee and Beatrice realize that their school was poorly equipped. Not having experienced anything else, they had nothing to compare it to, and besides, they were young and having fun. "Daisy Lee and I had the same wonderful teacher, Ruth Cox, for years," recalled Mrs. Epps, "and there was a store near school where we'd buy pickles and candy and eat them together while drinking soda pop."

Daisy's early childhood was happy. "Daddy" and "Mamma," as she called and thought of her adoptive parents, doted on her. She later described herself as somewhat spoiled and so skinny that Early Broughton, a cousin on Mamma's side of the family, insisted she was "all hair and legs." Daisy Lee was very athletic and liked to show off by climbing an old mulberry tree in back of her house. One day she took quite a spill out of the tree, landing on a piece of broken glass. After the doctor sewed up her knee, Daisy decided to stick to less-dangerous games and sports. She and Beatrice played baseball with the boys, jumped rope, and played hopscotch. Daisy also took up marbles, becoming so good that she won a whole boxful from her friends.

Once when a boy lost a favorite marble to Daisy—a fancy kind called an agate—he decided he wanted it back. Daisy's mother overheard the children arguing and came to investigate.

"Daisy, give him back his marble!" ordered Mamma, who was an extremely religious woman and a strict parent. "You know you're not supposed to play for keeps! That's gambling, and gambling is a sin."

When the other neighborhood children discovered how Daisy's mother felt about gambling, they came to retrieve the marbles they had lost. "Miss Susie," they said, "Daisy got our marbles."

Mamma made Daisy bring the shoebox where she stored her marbles. The other children were allowed to take the ones they had lost to Daisy, until she was left with only a few marbles.

Angry at being deprived of her winnings, Daisy pointed out that every Saturday night Daddy played poker with his friends—and *he* got to keep any money he won. That just earned her father a lecture at the dinner table. "Daisy has been playing marbles for keeps!" Mamma told Daddy. "You see what you're doing to your daughter—you and your Saturday night poker games!"

Daisy's and Beatrice's families belonged to the Sanctified Church, located right behind the Smiths' home. Officially known as the Church of God in Christ, the denomination had originated in Arkansas in 1895. Orlee Smith generally didn't go to church much, but after the marbles episode, Mamma made both Orlee and Daisy Lee go to Sunday services to ask the Lord to forgive them for gambling. One Sunday morning Daisy had an idea. "Daddy," she suggested, "why don't you go to church and ask God to forgive you for a whole month? Then you won't have to go to church every Sunday!"

Mamma gave Daisy Lee a spanking for that remark. On numerous occasions

Mamma also made her stand in the corner as punishment. Later Daisy Bates recalled that the corner floor became worn from all the hours she spent standing there.

Summer was Daisy's favorite season, for then she and her parents would visit relatives in other parts of Arkansas and in nearby states. Daisy especially loved her trips to see her adoptive grandmother—Susie Smith's mother—who had a farm in New Edinburg, Arkansas, about fifty miles north of Huttig. Daisy was very close to her grandmother, and she also liked to see her farm animals, which included a milk cow, pigs, a brown hound dog, and an old gray horse Daisy was allowed to ride.

Until she was seven years old, Daisy rarely thought about race. Ever since she could remember, black people had lived on one side of town and whites on the other. There was no reason for her to think things could be different. Also, as she wrote in her autobiography, "My parents, as do most Negro parents, protected me as long as possible from the inevitable insult and humiliation that is, in the South, a part of being 'colored.'"

Ironically, a white girl her own age was the first person to suggest to her that things might be different. Daisy and this girl had apparently met in Huttig's little business district—the place where people of both races most frequently crossed paths. Daisy and the white girl sometimes met at the commissary store. If either of them had a few pennies, she would buy candy and share it with the other. The two little girls looked through magazines at the store and talked about the faraway places they would like to visit together. In one magazine they found a picture of the Statue of Liberty and New York City. They were discussing what they would do if they could travel to New York together when suddenly Daisy's friend asked:

"Do you think it will always be like this? I can't come to your house and you can't come to mine."

Daisy didn't know what to say, for she hadn't yet questioned the way things were in Huttig.

Shortly after her seventh birthday, Daisy had her first serious encounter with prejudice. Her mother was not feeling well, so she asked Daisy to shop for her at the meat market next to the commissary.

Proud to be sent on such an important errand, Daisy put on a special dress and sat patiently as Mamma brushed her hair. Her mother then gave Daisy a dollar and told her to buy one pound of center-cut pork chops.

Inside the meat market Daisy took her place behind several white adults who were waiting their turn. After the adults were served, Daisy stepped up to the counter and asked the butcher for a pound of center-cut pork chops. In the meantime, though, other white adults had entered the market, and the butcher turned away from Daisy to fill their orders. Daisy was a little annoyed, but she figured the butcher had skipped her turn and served those people because they were adults.

The butcher was still waiting on the grownups when a white girl came into the store and took a place behind Daisy. The white girl and Daisy passed the time by talking. Finally, all the adults had been served and the butcher asked: "What do you want, little girl?"

Daisy smiled at the man and repeated her request for a pound of center-cut pork chops.

"I'm not talking to *you,*" the butcher answered Daisy in a disdainful tone. He wanted to know what the *white* girl wanted. As the butcher filled the other girl's order, it dawned on Daisy that he had served all these people ahead of her because she was black and they were white. She wanted to run out of the store, but her mother had sent her there to buy meat for supper, so she held back her tears and continued to wait.

Finally, Daisy was the only customer. "Please may I have my meat?" she asked.

The butcher grabbed Daisy's dollar, reached into the meat case, and pulled out a pound of the fattiest pork chops, which he wrapped in paper. Shoving the package at Daisy, he said with a scowl: "Niggers have to wait till I wait on the white people. Now take your meat and get out of here!"

Daisy, who had never been called "nigger" before, couldn't hold back her tears any longer. She took the package and ran home sobbing.

When her mother asked what was wrong, Daisy could barely get the words out. She repeated what the butcher had said, then unwrapped the package so that Mamma could see the fatty meat. "Let's take it back!" cried Daisy, growing angry now that she had reached the safety of home.

"Oh, Lord, I knew I shouldn't have sent her," Mamma said quietly. She tried to comfort Daisy by pretending that the meat wasn't so bad. As Daisy continued to cry, Mamma's eyes filled with tears too. "Go on out on the porch and wait for Daddy," she told her daughter.

Orlee Smith was a lumber grader at the sawmill—an important job that involved determining the quality of the lumber and what it should be used for. The moment she saw him coming, Daisy ran to her father, who lifted her up and asked why she was crying. Certain that he would take her back to the market and tell off the butcher, Daisy tearfully explained what had happened. She watched her father's smile disappear and felt his muscles become rigid. "We'll talk about it after dinner, sweetheart," he said, carrying her into the house.

Mamma had cooked the pork chops, which the three of them ate without their usual suppertime conversation. Observing the frustrated looks on her parents' faces, Daisy began to understand: They couldn't remedy the injustice that had been done to her.

African Americans had suffered countless injustices since first being brought to the American colonies three hundred years earlier. Back in slavery days, which lasted until about half a century before Daisy Lee's birth, African American slaves had been deprived of virtually every right enjoyed by Americans today. They hadn't been allowed to attend school, testify in court, have legal marriage ceremonies, own property, or even live with their children if their owners decided to separate a family. The ending of slavery after the Civil War in 1865, and the ratification of the 13th, 14th, and 15th Amendments to the Constitution between 1865 and 1870, were supposed to guarantee the civil rights of black citizens. But during the late 1800s and well into the 1900s, white southerners found ways to deprive the former slaves and their descendants of their rights as American citizens.

In the South black people weren't allowed to vote. Black children were sent to separate and inferior schools—if they were permitted to attend school at all. Black southerners had to ride in segregated train compartments, and they were banned from many facilities, ranging from parks to theaters, that were considered "whites only." Sometimes black people suffered discrimination by law, but often it was simply by custom. For example, black southerners were expected to move out of the

A segregated railroad station in the South.

way of whites on sidewalks—even if it meant going out into a muddy street. African Americans were also expected to say "Yes, sir" and "Yes, ma'am" to white people, but whites called blacks of every age by their first names, or by belittling words such as "boy." African Americans who defied these unjust laws or customs risked being beaten up or even murdered. Black southerners couldn't expect justice from the legal system, either, for they were kept off juries.

After supper Daisy's father took her aside and did his best to explain that black people had no rights that white people were obligated to respect. With tears in his eyes he dropped to his knees and said, "Can't you understand what I've been saying? There's nothing I can do! If I went down to the market I would only cause trouble for my family!"

That night Daisy went to bed with a troubled heart. She hated the butcher for what he had done, not only to herself but to her parents. Instead of her usual bedtime prayers, she prayed that the butcher would die—and she felt angry at herself for such thoughts.

Her parents never spoke to Daisy about the meat market incident again. But the occurrence was a turning point in her life, for it marked the end of her being protected from the "inevitable insult and humiliation" that came with being a black person in the South.

Forty Acre Pond.

3

"Who Killed My Mother?"

Looking back at her childhood in later life, Daisy realized she had long suspected that the couple she called "Mamma" and "Daddy" weren't her birth parents. For one thing, she didn't look like either of them. There were also remarks that she overheard.

For example, a traveling salesman who stopped by the house once quietly asked her mother: "Have you heard from her father?"

After Mamma said that she hadn't, the salesman looked toward Daisy and asked, "Does she know?"

"We haven't told her," Mamma answered. Daisy pretended to be unaware of their whispering, but she caught every word.

The fact was, Daisy didn't spend much time wondering about her background, for Mamma and Daddy had raised her and were the only parents she knew.

Then one day sometime around her eighth birthday, Daisy was playing with her friends on a neighbor's stoop when an older boy came by and began pulling her braids. When Daisy threatened to go home and tell Miss Susie, the boy said she wouldn't act so stuck up if she knew what had happened to her mother.

She had just left her mother a few minutes earlier and she was just fine, Daisy answered.

"I'm talking about your *real* mother," the boy continued, "the one the white man took out and killed."

Daisy called the boy a liar, but he insisted that he had heard his parents talking about it.

Daisy sensed that this was a subject her parents would not want to talk about—like the incident at the meat market. But just thinking about the possibility that her real mother had been murdered was so troubling to the third-grade girl that she became physically ill. Although Daisy didn't have a temperature, her parents made her swallow some little pink pills that may have been a patent medicine—an old-time nonprescription medicine that could supposedly cure a variety of ailments.

She had been thinking of little else besides her real mother for several weeks when her favorite cousin, Early Broughton, came to visit. A few years older than Daisy, Early B., as she called him, was a lot like an older brother, protecting her from the neighborhood bullies whenever he was around. Daisy and Early B. were walking near Forty Acre Pond one afternoon when she asked him to tell her about her mother.

With a puzzled look on his face, Early B. pointed to the house in the distance, where Mamma was sitting out on the porch.

"No, I mean my *real* mother," Daisy explained.

Early B. grew angry. He demanded to know who had told Daisy about her real mother, threatening to beat him up. Then he asked Daisy if she had discussed the subject with Mamma and Daddy. "No," she answered, scared and yet eager for Early B. to tell her what he knew.

Daisy's cousin told her the simple facts. When Daisy had been a baby, her real mother had been lured from home and killed by a white man she had known, possibly with the help of two other white men. In the morning Daisy's real father had returned home from work and found his daughter being watched by a neighbor and his wife missing. Later that morning fishermen discovered the body of Daisy's mother, half submerged in Forty Acre Pond. Someone identified the man or men involved in the murder, but the local authorities did little or nothing about it. Realizing that the murderers might go after him next, Daisy's father left her with his best friends, the Smiths, then fled to an unknown location.

After he finished the story, Early B. couldn't persuade Daisy to leave the pond with him. For hours she sat by herself staring into the dark water while thinking of ways to take revenge on her mother's killers.

The sun had set and it had grown dark when Daisy heard Daddy's voice say, "It's time to go home, darling." He reached out his hand, helped Daisy to her feet, and headed with her toward home. On the way he asked her how long she had known that he and Mamma weren't her real parents.

"A long time," she answered.

The next morning Daisy awoke with a high temperature. She felt delirious and slept on and off while people went in and out of her room. That afternoon a friend brought her a small box containing three guinea pigs as a get-well gift. Daisy was clearheaded enough to realize that her mother would object to her having the furry little animals, so she hid the box beneath her bedcovers.

In the evening some of Mamma's lady friends from church came to Daisy's home. They knelt around her bed and prayed for her to recover. Learning what had happened to her real parents had made Daisy angry at the world. Just to be mean, she lowered the box to the floor and released the guinea pigs near the knees of a woman who was praying by her bedside. One of the little animals scurried across the lady's leg. The woman began to scream. The scene might have been funny in one of the silent movies that were popular at the time, but in real life Daisy had done something cruel, and Mamma was embarrassed. Daisy Lee must have been feeling better by then, for her mother gave her a spanking for what she had done.

Daisy recovered from her illness, but not from her torment about her mother's murder. She became moody, crying at times for no apparent reason. For example, she had always loved flowers—having been named for one—and at a young age had begun to garden. She made many bouquets for people using flowers from her garden and wildflowers she found in the woods.

Early one morning Daisy went out to pick the last bouquet of the year from her yard but found that all the flowers had withered except one red rose. While she stared at the lone flower wet with dew, it suddenly occurred to her that nothing lasts forever. She ran into the house crying that all the other flowers had died and that her red rose would die too.

Orlee and Susie Smith finally realized that they had to talk to Daisy. On a Saturday afternoon Daddy asked her to go for a walk in the woods, saying he thought they might find some persimmons, a sweet, yellowish-orange fruit. Also, he knew a place in the woods where there was a large old walnut tree that might have some tasty nuts.

It was a crisp autumn day, and the smell of pine needles filled the air as the father and daughter entered the woods. After they had walked quite a way, they approached the persimmon grove, but Daisy knew that her father had taken her out to talk, so she quickly forgot about the persimmons and walnuts.

"Daddy," Daisy asked, "who killed my mother? Why did they kill her?"

The two of them sat down on some flat rocks on a hill, where Daddy spoke to his daughter almost as if she were an adult. He described her real mother's "beauty, her pride, her love for my father," Daisy later wrote. Then he told her the same basic story as Early B.

"They say that three white men did it," Daddy said, with intense bitterness in his voice. "There was some talk about who they were, but the sheriff's office did little to find out."

"When we walked out of the woods, Daddy looked tired and broken," Daisy wrote in her autobiography. "He took my hand and we walked home in silence."

Her father probably thought their talk hadn't helped Daisy, but it had. She wasn't alone in her feelings, she realized. Daddy was just as angry and frustrated about her real mother's death as she was.

The conversation changed Daisy in another way. No longer was she angry at the world. Her fury was focused on white people. It was they who made her people wait at the store, called them "nigger," and kept them in one part of town. It was they who had murdered her real mother and made Daddy and Mamma afraid. She began to view all white people with hatred and suspicion. Was that man sitting on the bench one of her mother's killers? Was that white child a murderer's son or daughter?

One day as Daisy was leaving the commissary, the white girl with whom she

The commissary.

had been friends came up from behind and gave her a playful poke. "Look, Daisy," she said, "I have two pennies. Let's buy some candy and I'll tell you about my vacation."

Before she could think, Daisy wheeled about and slapped the girl in the face. "Don't you ever touch me again!" Daisy said with hatred in her voice. "I don't want your penny!"

Seeing the girl's shocked expression, Daisy burst into tears and ran home. Mamma and Daddy weren't there, so she sat alone on the porch thinking about what she had done.

At first Daisy wanted to run back and tell the girl she was sorry. Then she remembered a story she had heard about a neighbor boy's encounter with a white girl in town. Approaching the boy on the sidewalk, the girl had said, "Get off the walk, nigger, and let me pass."

"You don't own the sidewalk!" the boy had answered, adding that he shouldn't have to go into the muddy street since the sidewalk was wide enough for both of them. Later, the girl and her father had appeared at the black boy's home. Pulling out a belt, the girl's father had ordered the boy's father to whip him, as a lesson to "respect white folks." Refusing would have meant trouble for his family, so the black boy's father had whipped him as ordered.

Daisy wondered: Would the father of the girl she had slapped come and make Daddy whip her? The more she thought about it, the more she realized that going to the commissary to apologize might just stir up trouble with the white people. Daisy stayed at home. She never told her parents that she had slapped her white friend, nor did she ever apologize to the girl. Although nothing more came of the incident, the friendship between Daisy and the white girl was over.

Her old friend Beatrice Cowser Epps remembers how Daisy began to stand up to white people at about this time. "We were walking down the sidewalk one time and I bumped into a big white guy who pushed me off the sidewalk. Daisy got mad and said, 'Why did you push her off the sidewalk?' She was like that, always speaking up. When she said things I thought she shouldn't say, I would elbow her to try and get her to hush, but Daisy was so brave."

Instead of avoiding the meat market, Daisy would go there and make comments. "We'd stand for hours at the meat market to get waited on," Beatrice continued. "I remember once when we were waiting a long time, Daisy said, 'Girl, it's a shame we've had to wait for all these people who came in after us.' Another time she said, 'Bea, this is so disgusting, it's pitiful.'" Beatrice believes that Daisy began standing up for her rights "because of what they did to her mother," and that her childhood acts of defiance marked her start as a civil rights fighter.

Her dislike of white people even changed her view of Christmas. At the age of seven Daisy had appeared in her church's yearly Christmas pageant. Dressed in an angel costume, Daisy had been a highlight of the show as she stood over the straw crib containing a doll that represented the Christ child. But when one of the church ladies came to ask if she would again play the part of an angel, eight-year-old Daisy angrily answered, "No, I *won't!*"

Mamma asked why she was so upset. "I don't want to be in the play about a dead white doll!" Daisy replied.

Susie Smith was deeply disturbed by her daughter's comments. "I won't have that kind of talk!" she warned.

But Daisy had more to say. "All the pictures I ever saw of Jesus were white!" she yelled. "If Jesus is like the white people, I don't want any part of him." Then she ran from the room.

Her parents said nothing more about the Christmas play to Daisy. While her family and friends attended the pageant, Daisy Lee stayed home and played with a little brown-colored doll Mamma and Daddy had gotten for her.

Lucius Christopher Bates.

4

"Hate Can Destroy You, Daisy"

Her friend Beatrice recalls that Daisy had a fun-loving side as they were growing up in Huttig. Their church had many strict rules. "They hated dancing. We couldn't play baseball, couldn't wear lipstick, couldn't wear our stockings rolled down, and we were supposed to wear our sleeves below our elbows," Beatrice explained. She and Daisy broke many of the rules, sometimes with the help of Orlee Smith.

"We lived about three blocks apart, and sometimes I'd sleep over at Daisy's house," Beatrice continued. "When Daisy's mother, Susie, would go to town, Daisy's father would get out the wind-up Victrola and put on records. He'd say, 'Go dance, girls, and if I see Miss Susie coming, I'll yell.' Daisy and I would dance—we'd do the Charleston, the Big Apple, the snakehips, and the peck." While describing these events of eighty years ago, Beatrice demonstrated the peck by moving her head back and forth like a chicken. "We'd dance until he would yell, 'Girls, girls, here comes Miss Susie, turn that Victrola off!'"

But inwardly Daisy was moody and often unhappy. She fantasized a great deal about taking revenge upon her real mother's killers. Since the commissary and the meat market were good places to observe white people, she went there whenever she could. She looked like her real mother, Daisy had been told. Eventually she would run into the murderers. They would recognize her as their victim's daughter, and Daisy would see the guilt written across their faces. Then she would find a way to punish them.

Daisy wanted everyone to know she was Millie Riley Gatson's child. Until learning about her birth mother, she had gone by the name Daisy Lee Smith. Now she began to call herself Daisy Lee Gatson.

One day, while entering the commissary with Beatrice, Daisy noticed a dirty-looking white man in rumpled clothes staring at her oddly from a bench outside the store. He seemed to be in some kind of daze, but as she stared back, Daisy thought she saw the man's expression change from bewilderment to fright.

Beatrice nudged her and said, "C'mon, Daisy Lee!" because staring at a white person could cause trouble. But Daisy continued to glare at the man until he rose unsteadily from the bench and staggered away. Beatrice asked what that had been about, but Daisy wouldn't say.

All the next day at school, Daisy thought about returning to the commissary to see if the dirty-looking white man was there. Rushing home from school, she asked Mamma if she needed anything from the store. Mamma didn't, so Daisy volunteered to do a little shopping for a neighbor.

As on the previous day, the man was sitting on the bench outside the commissary. When he looked at Daisy, she stared back with her meanest expression. "Stop staring at me, you bitch!" he shouted, jumping up from the bench and advancing toward her. Daisy was so scared she couldn't move, but the man stopped when he noticed an elderly black man looking on. In her autobiography Daisy Bates doesn't reveal the identity of the elderly man, but Beatrice Cowser Epps says that he was a retired mill worker named Irvin Stewart who used to give them candy. "Go away!" the white man yelled at Daisy, but she still didn't move. After a few moments he wandered away, muttering to himself.

Daisy felt frightened yet excited. The man was so drunk, he hardly knew where he was, Daisy overheard people at the store say, but she was sure that she had found one of her mother's murderers and that he was more scared of her than she was of him. She made up a name for him—"Drunken Pig"—and decided to dedicate herself to tormenting him.

Over the next few months she found excuses to visit the commissary three or four times a week. All day in school she planned the dirty looks she would give Drunken Pig when she saw him. After a while, instead of staring back, Drunken Pig tried to avoid Daisy's eyes. She enjoyed watching his mouth twitch as he pretended not to notice her.

With the passing weeks Drunken Pig became drunker and dirtier than before, and it gave her pleasure to think she was the cause. On a damp March afternoon she found Drunken Pig asleep on the bench. Daisy went into the store for a few minutes. Coming out, she saw that he still hadn't moved. Something prompted her to nudge him to see if he was still alive. He awoke slowly. As she looked into his eyes, Daisy couldn't help feeling sorry for him for an instant. Then he struggled to stand, and stumbled into the alley behind the commissary mumbling, "Leave me alone!"

The next few days were rainy and Daisy was housebound with a cold. As soon as she felt better, she headed to the commissary. Drunken Pig wasn't in his usual spot, nor was he inside the store or at the post office next door.

Irvin Stewart, the elderly black man who had witnessed a number of the staring contests, told Daisy that she wouldn't be seeing Drunken Pig anymore. When she asked why not, he answered that earlier in the day he had been found dead in the alley. To her amazement Daisy began crying and couldn't stop. "You're the only one in town to cry over that drunkard," old Mr. Stewart said quietly.

She walked home as if in a trance, pondering the fact that she had wanted Drunken Pig dead and now he really was. For the next few nights she went to sleep crying—whether because she no longer had Drunken Pig to torment or for some other reason she wasn't sure.

Hearing Daisy cry, Daddy entered her room one night and sat on a chair near her bed. "I know you've been unhappy for a long time," he said, taking her hand. "I talked with the old man who sits by the commissary. He told me about that drunk who died, and he said I should send you away. Do you want to tell me what it was about?"

Between her sobs Daisy explained that she believed Drunken Pig was one of her mother's murderers, and that she had been trying to torment him. Now that he was dead, she felt bad but didn't know why. Daisy never related what her father said to comfort her, and she never learned with any degree of certainty whether Drunken Pig had actually been connected with her mother's murder.

Although the killing of her birth mother would haunt Daisy all her life, she coped with it better after Drunken Pig's death. She began spending more time with her friends, including Beatrice, who recalls what the two of them were like at the age of twelve.

"We would put on lipstick and go uptown to the community house, which like everywhere else had blacks on one side and whites on the other. We'd sit in the community house drinking cherry Cokes, talking to guys, and thinking we were cute. We would also sneak off to the movie theater, where the whites sat downstairs and the blacks in the balcony."

In a small community like Huttig's Negro Town, everyone knew what everyone else was up to. Daisy's and Beatrice's behavior couldn't possibly go unnoticed, especially since their whole purpose was to *be* noticed. It became widely known at their church that Daisy Lee Gatson and Beatrice Cowser wore lipstick, dressed improperly, and flirted with boys.

"When Daisy and I were about twelve years old," Beatrice recalled, "we were thrown out of the Sanctified Church" for breaking so many of the rules. "We didn't care," she added, because it seemed to them that their church opposed everything that was fun.

Daisy may not have cared, but Mamma was humiliated by her daughter's expulsion from the church. By this time mother and daughter were often at odds over Daisy's behavior. They apparently had many fights over Daisy's sneaking out of the house to go uptown with Beatrice. Susie Smith was also upset that her husband encouraged what she considered to be Daisy's wild ways. Not only did he not try to stop her from wearing lipstick and flirting with boys at the community house, he often slipped her money so she could go off and have fun.

The mother-daughter arguments intensified as Daisy approached her teens. After Daisy graduated from eighth grade, things got so bad between them that Susie

Smith decided to send her thirteen-year-old daughter to live with her mother in New Edinburg, Arkansas. According to Beatrice, while Daisy was in New Edinburg for several years during the late 1920s, she attended a "colored high school" somewhere in the area. This enabled her to get more of an education than she could have had in Huttig, where schooling for black children ended after eighth grade. While living in New Edinburg, Daisy frequently visited Huttig to see her parents and friends, but she and her mother never completely patched up their differences.

It was back in Huttig that fifteen-year-old Daisy Lee Gatson met her future husband. Lucius Christopher Bates was a tall, thin insurance agent who stopped by to sell Daddy a policy. L.C. Bates and Daisy's father became friends. As he traveled his nine-state territory, L.C. began making regular visits to the Smith home, and Daisy always tried to be there when he stopped by.

Gradually she learned about L.C. Twelve years older than Daisy, he had been born in Liberty, Mississippi, on April 27, 1901. The son of a Baptist minister, L.C. had many advantages compared to most young black people of his time. His family provided him with an excellent education in hopes that he would become a physician, but as a youth growing up in Indianola, Mississippi, he landed a job as a "printer's devil"—an apprentice in a printer's shop. L.C. later claimed that he "got ink in his veins" while working in the printing office, because from then on his goal was to run his own newspaper.

After high school graduation L.C. went north to attend college in Ohio, but he was so eager to begin his journalism career that he dropped out after only a year. At nineteen he went to work for the *Interstate Reporter,* a black newspaper in Helena, Arkansas. Next came a stint in Missouri with the black-owned *Kansas City Call,* where he worked under Roy Wilkins, who would later head the NAACP.

At the age of twenty-two L.C. decided he was ready to begin a newspaper of his own. He moved to Pueblo, Colorado, where he lived at the YMCA and began the *Western Ideal.* His paper didn't last long, though, and after its demise L.C. went to California, where he worked for the *Golden Age,* a black newspaper in Los Angeles.

In 1924 he married Cassandra Crawford, with whom he settled in Memphis and had a daughter named Loretta. L.C. hadn't made much money in journalism, so about the time that he and Cassandra married, he left the newspaper business and went to work as an insurance agent. When he met Daisy in about 1928, L.C. had been an insurance agent for four years and was quite successful at it. However, his dream was to return to journalism, for he loved that profession and believed that nothing could help his people as much as a crusading newspaper. He also confided in Daisy that he and Cassandra weren't getting along and would eventually get divorced.

Daisy was intrigued by L.C.'s stories about the places he had been and his plans for returning to the newspaper business. Whenever he came to visit, he brought magazines and newspapers that weren't available in Huttig, as well as candy and other gifts for the family. Once he brought Daisy a bracelet.

Now and then L.C. invited Daisy and her parents to accompany him to Huttig's movie theater. One evening in the Negro section of the darkened theater, L.C. suddenly took Daisy's hand in his. "I was thrilled," she later wrote, "for I had grown to love and respect him during his visits." She paid little attention to what was on the screen the rest of the evening. Sitting in the theater that night in about 1929, Daisy made up her mind that she would one day marry L.C. Bates.

In her autobiography Daisy Bates describes the hand-holding scene in the Huttig movie theater, then skips to her marriage to L.C. She neglects to explain that she didn't marry L.C. until about 1941. What occurred during the twelve years between the time the couple fell in love and the time they got married?

Several people who knew Daisy Bates long ago can provide some answers. They include Daisy's friend Beatrice Cowser Epps, her cousin Clifton Broughton, and L.C.'s cousin Lottie Brown Neely. Although they don't always agree about dates and events, these three people helped us reconstruct the twelve "missing years" of Daisy's life.

By the early 1930s Daisy no longer lived at her grandmother's farm in New Edinburg and was back in Huttig. Sometime around 1932 L.C. asked Daisy to come live with him even though he was not yet divorced from Cassandra. Daisy liked the idea, but first she and L.C. discussed it with her parents.

Susie Smith considered it sinful for her daughter to run off with a married man, but Orlee Smith felt differently. By this time Daisy's father was in failing health. If he died, how would Mamma care for Daisy herself? Orlee also admired L.C., who was one of the most brilliant people he had ever met. Besides, L.C. promised that he would marry Daisy once he and Cassandra were divorced. L.C. later told his cousin Lottie what Orlee Smith said when he gave his approval for Daisy to go live with him:

"You can give her a better life than she has down here."

Orlee Smith apparently had the last word, because Daisy went off to live with L.C. Bates around 1932 or 1933. Clifton Broughton knows that Daisy left home permanently around then because he was born in 1927 and was five or six years old when his cousin left Huttig.

Still in the insurance business, L.C. spent much of his time driving through the nine states that comprised his territory. Daisy may have accompanied L.C. on some of his trips as he drove about selling insurance. When not on the road or making an occasional visit to Huttig, Daisy and L.C. lived in several different places. According to Beatrice, the couple lived at first in Shreveport, Louisiana, about 100 miles southwest of Huttig. Later they lived in Memphis, Tennessee, about 200 miles northeast of Huttig. Daisy probably had never completed high school, but while in Memphis, according to Beatrice, she took some classes at a local black college.

Orlee Smith was suffering from cancer, and by 1935 or 1936 he was extremely ill. One day Susie Smith called Daisy to tell her that Daddy was in a hospital in Alexandria, Louisiana. By the time Daisy arrived, the doctor informed her that her father wouldn't live much longer.

Mamma and Daisy took turns sitting with Orlee Smith. In the middle of the night, when her father was sleeping so peacefully that Daisy thought he might have lapsed into a coma, she began crying quietly. Her father opened his eyes and summoned the strength to talk to her one last time.

A "colored" drinking fountain in the South, late 1930s.

He said he was so ill that he looked forward to death. "I haven't much to leave you, Daisy, so come close and listen and remember what I have to say to you."

Daisy pulled her chair nearer to her father's bed and took his hand. He told her that he knew she hated white people and that he, too, had been mistreated by whites many times in his life. But he had some advice for her.

"You're filled with hatred," Daddy said. "Hate can destroy you, Daisy. Don't hate white people just because they're white. Hate the humiliations we live under in the South. Hate the discrimination that eats away at every black man and woman. Hate the insults. And then try to do something about it, or your hate won't spell a thing."

Soon her father stopped talking and Daisy let go of his hand. A few minutes later, when one of the Catholic sisters entered the room, Daisy spoke to her pleasantly. It marked the first time in years that she had spoken in a friendly way to a white person.

The sun was just rising when Daisy left the hospital. It was the last day of her father's life, she knew, but she didn't cry, for "I realized that he was at peace with himself," she later wrote. As she repeated his words in her head, she also knew that her father had left her some valuable advice:

Try to do something about it, or your hate won't spell a thing.

This photo was taken in 1935, when schools for black children near Little Rock did not open until January 1, after all the cotton had been picked.

5

Birth of the *Arkansas State Press*

Daisy didn't visit Huttig much after her father died. She and her mother still didn't get along. They had an especially big argument at the time of Orlee Smith's funeral, explains Daisy's cousin Clifton Broughton. A United States flag was displayed at the service for Orlee, who had been in the armed forces. Daisy and her mother argued about the flag—apparently over who would keep it. In addition, Susie Smith still felt that her daughter was living in sin. Three or four years had passed since Daisy had gone off with L.C., and he still hadn't divorced Cassandra.

In the late 1930s Daisy and L.C. moved to Little Rock, located in central Arkansas about 130 miles north of Huttig. The Arkansas capital was home to a large number of African Americans—roughly a quarter of its 85,000 people—at that time. As in other southern cities and towns, Little Rock's black citizens suffered from widespread discrimination.

Although some were teachers, carpenters, plumbers, barbers, and beauticians, and some owned their own businesses, most black Little Rockians had low-paying jobs. Men typically worked as waiters, janitors, garbage collectors, and bellhops, and women as laundresses, cooks, maids, and nannies for white households. To help their families get by, many black children shined shoes, delivered groceries, or sold newspapers and magazines on the streets.

Unlike many other southern communities, Little Rock had no laws prohibiting

35

the races from living in the same neighborhood. But according to custom, parts of the city were off-limits to African Americans. Many of Little Rock's black families lived in rundown buildings in poverty-stricken neighborhoods.

The city maintained a segregated educational system and poured far more resources into its white schools than into its black ones. By about 1940 Little Rock was spending $67 a year per white pupil but only $40 a year per black student. As a result, Little Rock's "colored schools" lacked playground space, up-to-date books, and sometimes teachers and classrooms. Clubs, sports teams, and musical activities in the black schools often had to be financed by the parents—a group already strapped for money. The Little Rock region was home to Philander Smith College and several other colleges for blacks. However, only white students were allowed in the Arkansas colleges that trained people for such professions as law, medicine, dentistry, pharmacy, and journalism.

Banned from hotels and restaurants in white areas, black Little Rockians were limited to their own "colored" dance halls, bars, and eating places on West Ninth Street and other black neighborhoods. Drinking fountains and bathrooms in the city's public places were labeled WHITE and COLORED. In addition, blacks weren't allowed to use the main branch of the Little Rock Public Library, and except for Fair Park, they were barred from most recreational facilities, including the city's zoo. On buses, black Little Rockians were supposed to sit in the back, or stand, rather than sit among the white passengers.

In 1940 L.C. invited his cousin Lottie Brown, a Mississippi native like himself, to move into the Little Rock rooming house where he and Daisy lived. At her home in Chicago in early 2003, Lottie Brown Neely described some of her memories of segregation in the Arkansas capital during the 1940s.

Shortly after her arrival in Little Rock, Lottie sat toward the front of a bus because the back of the vehicle was full. "Someone said, 'You must not be from down here,'" as a hint for her to stand, Mrs. Neely recalled. Rosa Parks's refusal to give up a seat in the white section of a bus in Montgomery, Alabama, was fifteen years in the future. Rather than cause trouble, Lottie stood, despite the fact that there were empty seats toward the front. "Back then you didn't go to white restaurants," Mrs. Neely continued, "and if you went to a theater, you had to sit in the back in the balcony." The exception was the Gem, a movie theater for Little Rock's black people.

The city's large black population convinced L.C. Bates that Little Rock was a good place to revive his dream. In 1940, after selling insurance for about sixteen years, he decided to start his own newspaper once more. He had invited his nineteen-year-old cousin Lottie to move in with him and Daisy so that she could assist with the paper.

The rooming house was already so crowded, Lottie remembers, that she had to sleep with the children of the establishment's owners. She also recalls the impression that L.C.'s twenty-seven-year-old girlfriend made on her.

"Daisy was a sweet, really nice person, and people just loved her. Children were crazy about Daisy, maybe because she acted childish, kidding around with them and playing with them and reading the comic pages from the newspaper to them.

"She was a very beautiful woman, about five feet four inches tall, with long, pretty hair. I liked the way she dressed—so up-to-date. She loved high-heeled shoes and beautiful clothes. She was generous—a person who would give you the clothes off her back. She called me her country cousin and gave me lots of her

Little Rock's West Ninth Street, about 1940.

THE POWER OF ONE

clothes. She loved to eat, especially fried greens and candied yams." But since Daisy disliked cooking, Lottie usually prepared food for the three of them.

At this point in life Daisy was more of what we would now call a "playgirl" than the civil rights leader she would later become. "She never had a childhood," explained Lottie Brown Neely, referring to Daisy's troubled earlier life, and she was determined to make up for it by having as much fun as possible. L.C. provided her with a car and lovely clothes. She had many friends her own age in Little Rock. Daisy spent her days reading and doing her hair and makeup, and her nights going out with her young friends when L.C. wasn't in town—and sometimes when he was.

Since they weren't married, Daisy didn't feel obligated to tell L.C. everything she did and with whom. "She was a flirt," Mrs. Neely continued. "She loved to flirt with guys. She'd go riding in L.C.'s car with her friends. L.C. would tell her what time to get back. If she felt that L.C. was treating her like a child, she'd get mad and sometimes throw a saucer or plate at his head. It tickled me because she was a good aim. I'd ask, 'L.C., what happened to your face?' He'd say, 'Oh, I ran into the door.'"

Finally, L.C. and Cassandra were divorced, and after nearly ten years of living together, he and Daisy married. Like that of her birth, the date of Daisy's marriage is unclear. L.C. claimed it was sometime in 1940, but his cousin Lottie thinks it was 1941. There was no big wedding party. "They just slipped away and got married," Lottie Neely explained. Later in life L.C. revealed to an interviewer that he and Daisy had been married by a justice of the peace in Fordyce, Arkansas. Daisy probably chose that location because Fordyce is just a few miles from New Edinburg, making it easier for her grandmother to attend the ceremony. Whether Susie Smith witnessed her daughter's wedding is unknown.

Nineteen forty-one was also when L.C. reentered the newspaper business, with Daisy as his partner. Daisy apparently had some money of her own, which L.C. wanted her to invest in the paper. Many years later, in her old age, Daisy Bates claimed that she agreed to help her husband start the newspaper only if it would "stand for something and not be one of those 'Negro papers' with a don't rock the boat attitude." More than a little annoyed at her, L.C. responded, "Why do you think I want to start a newspaper in the first place?"

The couple rented the office of a floundering black newspaper and began their own weekly paper, the *Arkansas State Press*. L.C. coined the paper's statement of purpose, which appeared on its editorial page:

THE DAY WE HOPE FOR

When we can live in peace and harmony with one another, irrespective of race, color, creed. . . . When that day arrives we will be contented. THEN, we all can boast of our DEMOCRACY, and NOT until then.

L.C. BATES

From its first issue, which appeared on Friday, May 9, 1941, the *State Press* offered national and local news of interest to African Americans, with an emphasis on civil rights matters. L.C. was the editor and main writer. Many of the people he had met during his years as a traveling insurance salesman became his customers as well as his sources for news.

"The newspaper became L.C.'s whole life," Lottie Neely recalled. "He sometimes worked until one or two o'clock in the morning, stopping only to eat a sandwich from a restaurant near the office of the *State Press,*" which was published at 923 West Ninth Street. Lottie worked alongside her cousin for four years, from 1941 to 1945. She was the newspaper's proofreader, which meant that she read the copy and corrected mistakes before the final version was printed.

"I had always been good with a camera," Lottie added, "so L.C. also sent me out to take pictures for the newspaper. When L.C. and Daisy were just starting out, they didn't have money to pay me, but later I was paid twelve and then fifteen dollars a week." Considering that L.C. covered his cousin's living expenses at the rooming house, this wasn't a bad salary for the early 1940s.

And what about Daisy Bates, L.C.'s wife and partner on the newspaper? At first, says Lottie Neely, Daisy didn't have much to do with the newspaper. L.C. was a seasoned journalist and twelve years older than she, so for a while Daisy lacked the confidence and desire to intrude on his domain.

Young black soldiers training for action in World War II.

6

"Do Something"

At first Daisy Bates did little more than keep the staff company in the newspaper office and get food for them at a nearby restaurant. But as she watched L.C., Lottie, and the handful of others at work, Daisy felt left out and began to seek a more active role with the *State Press*.

"She was good at thinking of ways to sell the paper," Lottie Neely explained. "She could think of ways that wouldn't occur to L.C." Daisy must have had some very good ideas, for within months the paper's circulation was 10,000—remarkable in a city with a black population only about twice that. Over time the *State Press* became the largest and most important African American newspaper in Arkansas, and one of the most influential black papers in the country. Its circulation eventually reached 22,000, including many white subscribers and a thousand readers outside Arkansas.

But Daisy wanted to do more than suggest ways to promote the *State Press,* which was sold both by subscription and by newsboys on the streets. She wanted to help create the paper. Just reading L.C.'s articles and discussing events with him provided her with a journalistic education. Having taken some college courses in Memphis, she was also a capable writer. She began by writing articles about the social news in Little Rock's black community: events such as weddings and special celebrations. By 1942 it was her habit to carry a notebook with her in case she came across a news story. She would share her information with L.C., who would help her write an article if he considered the story newsworthy.

Also by 1942 L.C. had begun the paper's first major civil rights campaign. "Negroes were beaten unmercifully by the city police at the slightest provocation," Daisy Bates wrote in her autobiography. "This seemed the most urgent cause to which we should devote our first crusade. The campaign against police brutality went on relentlessly but fruitlessly until a series of local events enabled us to make a real breakthrough."

The most notorious of these "local events" was the shooting of a black soldier in Little Rock in March of 1942. Three months earlier, in December of 1941, the United States had entered World War II. This conflict, which would be the bloodiest war ever fought, pitted Great Britain, France, the United States, and the other Allies against Germany, Japan, Italy, and the other Axis powers. Among the more than sixteen million Americans in uniform were more than a million African Americans, who generally served in all-black units.

During the war thousands of black soldiers were stationed at military bases across the South, including Camp Robinson near Little Rock. Many of these black troops were from the North, and were unaccustomed to the discrimination that was an everyday fact of life for southern blacks. Besides, they were serving their country and expected to be treated civilly. But whenever they left their barracks and entered a city, the black troops risked getting into trouble for such "offenses" as "talking back" to whites who called them names, not making way for whites on sidewalks, or refusing to ride in the backs of buses. Local police forces usually sided with the white people in these disputes and in some cases beat up the black soldiers.

Trouble repeatedly erupted between the black troops stationed at Camp Robinson and Little Rock police and citizens. On Sunday, March 22, 1942, Private Albert Glover, a black soldier in Little Rock on a weekend pass, got drunk in the West Ninth Street area. When two white military policemen had difficulty getting him to return to Camp Robinson, two white Little Rock policemen stepped in. They beat Private Glover so brutally with their nightsticks that his head gushed blood and he had to be taken to a first-aid station.

The fight had attracted about four hundred onlookers, most of them black. Sergeant Thomas P. Foster, a black soldier from North Carolina, made his way through the crowd. He had been authorized to handle problems involving black soldiers from the base, Sergeant Foster insisted, and told the two white military policemen that Private Glover had been handled too roughly. The military policemen then grabbed and tried to arrest Foster. When Sergeant Foster fought back, Abner J. Hay, one of the Little Rock policemen who had beaten Glover, entered the scuffle and helped overpower him. As Sergeant Foster lay on the ground, Officer Hay suddenly aimed his gun at him and fired five shots. Officer Hay then lit his pipe and blew smoke over Sergeant Foster, who lay dying of bullet wounds to the stomach.

Meanwhile, Daisy Bates had been informed of the shooting and arrived at the scene just before an ambulance came to take Sergeant Foster to the hospital. Standing on the street next to Mrs. Bates was a black soldier who looked on with tears streaming down his face. Frustrated beyond endurance, he hurled his Army cap to the ground and stomped on it furiously. "Why should we go over there and fight?" he asked. "These are the sons of bitches we should be fighting!"

Fearing a riot, Little Rock policemen poured into the West Ninth Street district to disperse the angry crowd. Sergeant Foster died at the hospital several hours after having been shot. By then Daisy Bates had rushed back to the *State Press* office with her notes. With L.C.'s help, she wrote what may have been her first important article for the *State Press:*

CITY PATROLMAN SHOOTS NEGRO SOLDIER
Body Riddled While Lying on Ground
White Military Police Look On;
Brandishing Guns to Hold Crowd Back

One of the most bestial murders in the annals of Little Rock was witnessed Sunday afternoon at 5:45 at Ninth and Gaines streets, by hundreds of witnesses, when patrolman A. J. Hay shot and mortally wounded Sergeant Thomas P. Foster, member of Company D, 92nd Engineers, stationed at Camp Robinson, which is near by.

According to over a hundred eye witnesses, Sergeant Foster was shot five times while lying on the ground where he was knocked down and out by Military Police after trying to defend himself from the attack of Policeman Hay, who had exceeded his authority by interfering with Military Police prisoners. . . .

City Patrolman Shoots Negro Soldier. Article in the March 27, 1942, *Arkansas State Press*.

CITY PATROLMAN SHOOTS NE

Body Riddled While Lying On Ground

White Military Police Look On;
Brandishing Guns to Hold Crowd Back

ARKANSAS State Pres

VOLUME 12, NUMBER 39 LITTLE ROCK, ARKANSAS FRIDAY, MARCH 27, 1942 PRI

One of the most sensational murders in the annals of Little Rock tragedies was witnessed Sunday afternoon at 3:45 o'clock at Ninth and Gaines Streets, by hundreds of eye witnesses, when Patrolman A. J. Hay shot and mortally wounded Sergeant Thomas P. Foster, member of Company D, 92nd Engineers, stationed at Camp Robinson, which is near by.

According to over a hundred eye witnesses, Sergeant Foster was shot five times while lying on the ground where he was knocked down and out by Military police after trying to defend himself from the attack of policeman Hay, who had exceeded his authority by interfering with Military Police prisoners.

Lacerates Another Soldier

It is reliably reported that only a few minutes previous to the unmerciful killing of Sgt. Foster, Policeman Hay had attacked another soldier, who was identified as Pvt. Albert Glover, member of Company D. 92nd Engineers, who had been ordered out of town by Military Police for being intoxicated. According to a release in the papers, Glover admits being drunk, and further admits that he didn't remember very well what happened, but eye witnesses state clearly that Glover was hit by the civilian police and that Sgt. Foster inquired of the MPs why they gave the privilege of interfering to civilian police, when they were there to take care of the boys. The inquiry increased contempt for the soldiers in the eyes of the civilian policeman, and he was heard to ask Sgt. Foster, "What you got

SGT. THOMAS P. FOSTER

Gaines and Rev. J. F. Clarke of Pine Bluff.

At this meeting a committee

Editors Disagree Over War Is

NEW YORK, March 26 (ANP)—The degree to which the Negro people should give all out support to the fight against fascism abroad, proved to be the principal issue in the Schomburg collection's forum on "Publishing Negro News" last Thursday. Eugene Gordon, of the Daily Worker, the only daily newspaper in New York which employs Negroes on its editorial staff, opened the argument by declaring that the Negro press should consider Hitler and the Japanese as the main enemy and that the foes of the Negro in this country should be considered as secondary.

Mr. Gordon sharply criticized the "Double V" campaign of the Pittsburgh Courier and similar slogans of other newspapers. Ludlow Werner of the New York Age, Julius Adams of the Amsterdam Star-News and St. Claire Bourne, of the People's Voice, disagreed with Gordon. In different words, these three editors said that unless the Negro fought for and received democracy at home he would be in no position to defend it abroad.

Tom O'Connor of the New York daily, PM, indicated how difficult it was for PM in pushing through its twin policy of winning the war and fighting for Negro rights to draw the line whenever the campaign for Negro rights conflicted

with the war effort.

All of the newspaper men agreed that the Negro press was necessary; that its long tradition of struggle from 1827 to present day is glorious; that the Negro press has become an important American institution, and that newspapers like PM and the Daily Worker are most valuable in that they are read by the general American public to which the Negro press as yet does not have access.

This forum on the Negro newspaper and news in the daily press was the last of this season's Evenings with Negro authors. Francis R. St. John, chief of circulation department of the New York Public library, received an ovation from the crowd.

Dunbar Students Adopt New S

THE STUDENT body of Dunbar Junior impetus to the Negro's efforts in this a display of Democracy in his own land fighting to retain Democracy in America, ber Sergeant Thomas P. Foster.

Sgt. Foster was brutally murdered noon in front of a Negro church on Ga Sts. by Patrolman A. J. Hay, a white civ

Wilkie Pleads Recognition Of Negro In The

NEW YORK, Mar. 26 (ANP)—Speak gural dinner of Freedom house here last dell L. Wilkie, 1940 Republican preside urged that the color bar be eliminated in es navy to permit the enlistment of Negro mess attendants.

The day after the incident, Little Rock authorities began investigating Sergeant Foster's death. At the time, white law officers in the South were rarely punished for beating up or shooting blacks, regardless of the circumstances. Within three days city officials concluded that because Sergeant Foster had resisted arrest, Officer Hay's action was "justifiable." There was no mention of the fact that Foster had been objecting to the rough treatment of a fellow soldier, or that he had been lying half conscious on the pavement when Hay shot him repeatedly. By Thursday, March 26, 1942, Little Rock authorities considered the Foster shooting case closed.

Since the *State Press* came out once a week, Daisy and L.C.'s "City Patrolman Shoots Negro Soldier" article didn't appear until Friday, March 27. Highly critical of the "investigation" by Little Rock authorities, the *State Press* called for the city's black leaders to look into the case themselves. The events of the next few months introduced Daisy to the power of the press.

Due largely to *State Press* prodding, the Negro Citizens' Committee was formed to investigate the Foster case. On March 29—one week after the shooting—the committee announced its findings at Little Rock's First Baptist Church. That Sunday, black people from across Arkansas poured into the church to hear the committee call the killing "unjustifiable" because Hay had shot Foster five times "while he lay helpless on the ground." The Negro Citizens' Committee report was sent to the mayor of Little Rock, the commander of Camp Robinson, U.S. Secretary of War Henry Stimson, and President Franklin D. Roosevelt. The NAACP, which had been founded in 1909 to fight for black people's rights, added its voice to the protests about the Foster shooting.

Under mounting pressure two major governmental departments looked into the case. The U.S. Department of Justice concluded that the shooting had been "far from justifiable," while the U.S. Department of War insisted that soldiers of every color deserved "protection when on a pass in a civilian community."

Late in 1942 Officer Hay was brought before a federal grand jury in Little Rock, which was to decide whether there was enough evidence to charge him with a crime. Francis Biddle, the Attorney General of the United States (head of the

Two women decorate a grave in a Negro section of Arlington National Cemetery, 1943.

Department of Justice) sent a special assistant to handle the case. Black people packed the courtroom in hopes of seeing justice served. They were bitterly disappointed. Grand jury indictments are made by a majority vote. Of the twenty-three members of the federal grand jury in Little Rock, only three were black. That probably was a major factor in the grand jury's decision not to charge Officer Hay with a crime by a nineteen-to-four vote.

Meanwhile, the *State Press* had stirred up so much anger in the black community that white storekeepers were losing business. Blaming the Bateses, some of these businessmen canceled their advertising in the *State Press*. The newspaper suffered, for it depended on revenue from white as well as black advertisers. When the Bateses refused to end their crusade against police brutality, some Little Rockians tried a different approach. They offered L.C. a bribe to change his stance, but that didn't work, either.

"Let's face it," Daisy told her husband at a point when things appeared especially bleak, "we can't operate without advertisers."

"Things aren't that bad, Daisy," L.C. answered. "We still have our savings."

"And after that's gone, then what?" Daisy asked.

They still could make nickels and dimes selling the *State Press* to the people, L.C. answered. "We won't get rich, but at least we'll be able to make a living. And what's more, we'll publish an independent paper."

The couple continued their newspaper crusade against police brutality, arguing that hiring black policemen would ease the problem. The Bateses' relentless campaign soon led to the hiring of Little Rock's first black police officers. L.C. was also proved right about the newspaper's future. Its circulation kept climbing, and although it had to do without some big advertisers, a number of smaller businesses began to run ads in the paper.

As she became more involved with the newspaper, Daisy began to feel that she had "ink in her veins" like her husband. Through the *State Press* she could do what her father had advised—"do something" about discrimination. In 1945 L.C.'s cousin Lottie moved back home to Mississippi. When L.C. took a vacation in the spring of 1946, he had enough confidence in Daisy to leave her in charge of the newspaper as editor-in-chief. During the four weeks that L.C. was gone, Daisy covered several big stories.

The biggest involved a murder at the Southern Cotton Oil Mill, located a mile from the *State Press* office. Striking mill workers had been picketing the plant in four-man shifts. The company hired new workers to replace the employees who were on strike, and there was a fight on the picket line. Otha Williams, a strikebreaker, killed a black picketer named Walter Campbell.

Otha Williams was charged with murder but acquitted. The three black men who had been picketing with Campbell were also arrested and, for having tried to keep Otha Williams out of the mill, charged with breaking Arkansas's "right-to-work law." The trial of the three black men took place in the courtroom of Lawrence C. Auten, presiding judge of the First Division of the Circuit Court of Pulaski County (the county in which Little Rock is located). They were found guilty of "by force and violence, preventing Otha Williams from engaging in a lawful occupation." On March 23, 1946, each of the three black defendants was sentenced to a year in prison.

The bottom line was that a striking black worker had been killed, and

Arkansas's legal system had made the killer seem to be the victim. Like thousands of other African Americans, Daisy Bates was enraged. She sat down at her typewriter and wrote a furious article criticizing the judge, jury, and Arkansas law that had led to the conviction of the three black men.

L.C. returned from his trip before his wife's article was printed. When he read what she had written, he said, "Daisy, this is a pretty strong story. Do you realize that Judge Auten is one of the most powerful men in the state?"

Daisy had learned from her husband the importance of standing up for what was right, and she insisted that her article not be softened. It appeared in the *State Press* on March 29, 1946:

STRIKERS SENTENCED TO PEN
BY A HAND-PICKED JURY

Three strikers, who by all observations were guilty of no greater crime than walking on a picket line, were sentenced to one year in the penitentiary by a "hand-picked" jury, while a scab who killed a striker is free.

The prosecution was hard pressed to make a case until Judge Lawrence C. Auten instructed the jury that the pickets could be found guilty if they aided or assisted, or just stood idly by while violence occurred. There were no Negroes on the jury.

On April 25, a month after Daisy's article appeared, two Pulaski County deputy sheriffs came to the Bateses' door. "We have a warrant for your arrest," said one of them, handing the couple a document. It ordered that "L.C. Bates and Mrs. L. Christopher Bates, City Editors of the *Arkansas State Press,*" be arrested for "contempt of court." They were charged with criticizing Judge Lawrence C. Auten and his court in their newspaper.

Daisy and L.C. were fingerprinted and police photographs were taken of them. They were then allowed to post bail so they wouldn't have to remain in jail. Elmer

Schoggen and Ross Robley, two lawyers who also represented the striking workers at the Southern Cotton Oil Mill, agreed to represent the Bateses in court.

The couple's trial took place on April 29, 1946. It was held in the worst possible place for them—the courtroom of the judge Daisy had criticized in her article, Lawrence C. Auten. Judge Auten told the Bateses that "the article in the *State Press* implied that the entire court was dishonest and carried an implication that these men [the black strikers] were railroaded to the penitentiary." He sentenced L.C. and Daisy Bates to ten days in jail and fined them $100 apiece.

The husband and wife spent less than a day in jail, for the Arkansas Supreme Court ordered that each of them could be released on $500 bail. The couple posted bail and were free once more. The Arkansas Supreme Court also agreed to hear their appeal. The results of this hearing are now part of the Daisy Bates Papers at the Wisconsin Historical Society in Madison, Wisconsin.

The Bateses' attorneys, Schoggen and Robley, made a dramatic appeal to the highest court in Arkansas. "It makes no difference that they are members of a subordinate race," they argued. "The law is the same because of the Fourteenth Amendment to the Constitution of the United States." Passed in 1868, this amendment guaranteed civil rights to all U.S. citizens, including former slaves. Although white southerners had ignored the amendment for the better part of a century, it was still in force, at least theoretically.

Schoggen and Robley then hammered away at the fact that Judge Auten's decision had violated one of America's most cherished freedoms: freedom of the press as protected by the First Amendment to the U.S. Constitution. "A free press and an independent judiciary are necessary to a free society," they pointed out. "The peoples of America will remain free only so long as our press has the power to criticize fairly and justly."

The state Supreme Court handed down its decision on November 11, 1946. All charges against the Bateses were dismissed. In explaining the decision, Arkansas Supreme Court Chief Justice Griffin Smith made it clear that not just the U.S. Constitution but the Arkansas state constitution guaranteed freedom of the press.

Daisy and L.C. Bates had won an important victory not only for themselves, but

Daisy and L.C. Bates.

for all American journalists. Despite the seriousness of the matter, L.C. retained his sense of humor. Since the whole thing had begun with an article Daisy had written in his absence, he joked with the *State Press*'s office secretary that in the future he would think twice about taking a vacation.

As for Daisy Bates, the Arkansas Supreme Court victory was a milestone in her life. Besides boosting her confidence as a newspaperwoman, the episode taught her that it was possible to win against powerful forces if she kept fighting. Now thirty-three years old, Daisy had come a long way from the days when she had been a depressed eight-year-old girl in Huttig or a young woman interested only in going out riding with her friends in Little Rock.

She would have been amazed had she known where the next few years would take her.

"Colored" water cooler in an Oklahoma City, Oklahoma, streetcar terminal, 1939.

7

"There Must Be Some Place in America"

Their 1946 Arkansas Supreme Court triumph helped make L.C. and Daisy Bates two of the best-known black journalists in the South. The couple waged a number of crusades through their newspaper in the 1940s and 1950s. They campaigned to improve housing and city services for black Arkansans. They fought injustice in courtrooms and worked to open job and educational opportunities for their people. Progress was slow, but it came, thanks partly to the *State Press*.

Under threat of legal action the University of Arkansas at Fayetteville in the northwestern part of the state began admitting black students in 1948. Unfortunately, health problems connected to his wartime service caused the first black law student, Silas Hunt, to withdraw. To discourage other blacks from enrolling, university officials concocted an unusual way to segregate the next black law student, Jackie Shropshire: They fenced him off from his white classmates with a wooden railing! But his classmates objected, the railing was junked, and in 1951 Shropshire became the first African American to graduate from the University of Arkansas. Other black students followed, including Wiley Branton, who as an attorney would play an important part in Daisy Bates's later life.

In January 1951 the Little Rock Public Library Board voted to admit "Negroes beginning with students of the seventh grade" to the main library, although younger black children had to use a small branch library stocked with old,

53

outdated books until 1963. Around the early 1950s the Little Rock Zoo began to admit black visitors—but only on Thursdays. Also around that time downtown hotels began allowing organizations with black members to use their meeting rooms and permitting visiting sports teams with black players to stay overnight. However, the hotels continued to ban black individuals and families from renting their rooms. And while some facilities removed their WHITE and COLORED signs from drinking fountains, bathrooms remained strictly segregated.

These breakthroughs didn't make much of a dent in segregation, as a young black Army veteran from Little Rock learned. The veteran, who had just returned home after serving his country for four years during World War II, was so upset by how he was treated in his own hometown that he had to tell someone. He stopped by the *State Press* office to talk to Daisy Bates.

"Being home isn't as pleasant as I had thought," he sadly told her. In the Army, he explained, he had been judged on his merits and had risen to the rank of captain. Upon coming home to Little Rock, he had gone into a store to buy clothes. Instead of waiting on him politely, the sales clerk had said: "What do you want, boy?" He had walked out of the store in a rage.

Still stinging from being called "boy" at the clothing store, he had entered a restaurant without thinking. He was just about to sit down when he noticed that everyone in the room had stopped talking and was staring at him. Suddenly, he realized he had been away so long, he had forgotten about whites-only restaurants. "Pardon me," he had said, and walked out.

"I'm leaving the South," the young Army captain told Daisy Bates. "There must be some place in America where a Negro can be a man."

The Bateses felt that white leaders often made small concessions to avoid making more significant changes. They admitted a few blacks to the University of Arkansas while continuing to segregate thousands of black schoolchildren. Hotels opened their doors to a few blacks while continuing to keep the majority out. Because L.C. and Daisy saw the larger issues involved, the *State Press* sometimes adopted views that were unpopular with its readers.

For example, in 1949 Little Rockians voted to spend $359,000 to build a park for black people. That was quite a sum—the equivalent of nearly $3 million in today's money. The *State Press* opposed the project, partly because a new park for blacks would just continue segregation in the city. "In this day and time when the entire country is planning programs to stamp out segregation," the *State Press* declared, "it seems a little ironical that Little Rock Negroes should be [pleased about] the outmoded principles" of a segregated park. But the park was built, and Little Rock's recreational facilities remained for the most part segregated.

By the late 1940s Daisy Bates wanted to get closer to the front lines in the civil rights struggle. For a few years she and L.C. had been active in the NAACP, which had

This 1949 Bill Mauldin drawing illustrates some of the restrictions black veterans faced.

branches in Little Rock and a number of other Arkansas cities and towns. She felt that the leaders of the NAACP's Little Rock branch weren't doing enough to combat discrimination, so in 1948 she formed a group of about fifty people and attempted to start a Pulaski County chapter of the NAACP, with herself as president. The NAACP's national office in New York City rejected her application, because Pulaski County already had an NAACP branch in Little Rock.

Undaunted, she set her sights even higher. In 1952 Daisy Bates decided to run for president of the NAACP for the entire state of Arkansas. Some older black leaders insisted that she was too militant and would cause trouble. One warned that she might "go off the deep end at times" pursuing justice for her people. Nonetheless, Mrs. Bates had such a fine reputation in Arkansas through her newspaper work that no one dared run against her.

At the age of thirty-nine Daisy Bates was copublisher of Arkansas's largest black newspaper as well as president of the leading black organization in the state.

Little Rock's Central High School.

8

"You Will Refrain from Calling Me Daisy"

As the years passed, Daisy Bates found that her father's words were true: Discrimination and bigotry, not white people, were the enemies. In fact, by the 1950s many white people who believed in fair play and equality had joined the NAACP and other civil rights groups, and Daisy and L.C. had some white friends. In the mid-1950s the couple moved into a home at 1207 West 28 Street in a predominantly white neighborhood.

During her first few years as state NAACP president, however, Mrs. Bates achieved less than she had wanted. One reason was Arkansas's small NAACP membership: only 2,000 people in the 1950s. Another was that powerful forces opposed civil rights progress. The majority of southern politicians, business leaders, clergymen, and newspapers either favored the system of discrimination that had long been in place or remained silent about it.

For example, Mrs. Bates established cordial relations with Francis Cherry, who was Arkansas governor from 1953 to 1955. On December 30, 1953, Governor Cherry sent her a letter saying he had carried out her suggestions for improving the Negro Boys' Industrial School outside Little Rock. But neither Governor Cherry nor any other southern leader had any plans to integrate schools.

Then in 1954 something happened that appeared to be a turning point in the civil rights movement. On May 17 the United States Supreme Court handed down its decision *Brown v. Board of Education of Topeka,* a case that NAACP lawyer Thurgood Marshall had argued. The nation's highest court unanimously declared that segregation in the nation's public schools violated the federal Constitution and must end. This meant that a school system that automatically funneled all its black children into one school and all its white children into another was breaking the law.

School integration would lead to better race relations generally, Daisy Bates and other black leaders hoped. A major reason for bigotry was that the races didn't know each other. Black and white youngsters who attended school together were likely to get along better and accept each other as equals later in life.

Those who wanted school segregation to continue found a loophole in the Supreme Court's decision. The high court hadn't said exactly *when* schools must integrate. What was to prevent a district from taking five, ten, or even twenty years to integrate its schools? On May 31, 1955, the U.S. Supreme Court tried to clarify this with its *Brown II* decision. Districts must make a "prompt and reasonable start" to integrate their schools "with all deliberate speed," said the high court. This still didn't solve the problem, for "prompt and reasonable" could be interpreted various ways.

Some states began integrating their schools quickly. By the spring of 1957 Delaware, Kentucky, Maryland, Missouri, Oklahoma, West Virginia, and the District of Columbia had made considerable progress at school integration. But in Mississippi, where Senator James Eastland called the decision to send black and white children to the same schools a "monstrous crime," there was no progress as yet. The same was true of Georgia, where Governor Herman Talmadge claimed that school integration would lead to marriage between the races, which was still illegal in many states. Other southern states with little or no progress included Alabama, Florida, Louisiana, North Carolina, South Carolina, and Virginia. Tennessee, Texas, and Arkansas made some progress within the first three years of the 1954 Supreme Court ruling.

In Arkansas, Governor Francis Cherry said that his state would "obey the law" and begin school integration promptly. One of the first Arkansas towns to do so

NAACP lawyer Thurgood Marshall reading to his son.

was Hoxie, in the northeastern part of the state. According to an NAACP report in the Daisy Bates Papers at the Wisconsin Historical Society, Hoxie in 1955 had 1,284 people, including fourteen black families. The town maintained a "newer structure with adequate facilities" for its white students. On the other hand, the "Negro school" for the town's twenty-seven black elementary students had "outdoor toilets, a wood-burning stove, no janitor (the children did the janitorial work), and broken windows with leaking roof. During rainy weather, it was necessary for the children to wear boots to school in order to get in." Furthermore, one teacher had to deal with all the elementary grades, and graduates of the school seeking further education had to travel twenty-five miles to a black high school in Jonesboro, Arkansas.

On June 25, 1955, the Hoxie School Board voted to integrate its schools, mainly because the town lacked the money to continue operating separate schools for the races. Hoxie children attended school in the summer but had vacation later in the year so that they could help their families with the farm harvest. Integrated classes began on July 11. This posed no problems among Hoxie's children, who, according to the NAACP report, "played and attended classes together without incident."

However, on August 3, 1955, white adult racists from Arkansas and nearby states staged a rally in Hoxie. About two hundred people attended this meeting, at which speakers urged parents to remove their children from school until segregation was reinstituted. A number of parents did so, but according to the NAACP report the children began "slipping away and returning to school after their parents had removed them." By their simple desire to attend school, the children of Hoxie foiled the racists. The Hoxie School Board then obtained a court order to prevent racists from interfering with their schools, and integration proceeded peacefully. Other Arkansas towns where school integration was soon achieved included Fayetteville, Charleston, and Benton.

But what about Little Rock, the state's capital and largest city?

As her state's NAACP president, Daisy Bates began meeting with Arkansas lawmakers and school officials in 1954. On May 21, just four days after the original *Brown* decision, Little Rock Superintendent of Schools Virgil T. Blossom met with black leaders to explain how the city would respond to the Supreme Court ruling. L.C. came to this meeting, but his wife did not. At that time many people considered the NAACP and Daisy Bates too militant, while L.C. probably attended the meeting as a newspaperman.

L.C. and the black leaders arrived at the meeting feeling optimistic, but their hopes were quickly dashed. Little Rock would integrate its schools slowly, Mr. Blossom declared. When the superintendent finished speaking, L.C. Bates angrily rose to his feet. "Then the Board does not intend to integrate the schools in nineteen fifty-four?" he demanded to know.

"No, it must be done slowly," Mr. Blossom repeated.

L.C. Bates stormed out of the meeting. The *State Press* began criticizing Superintendent Blossom and the Little Rock School Board, accusing them of dragging their feet on integration.

In his autobiography, *It Has Happened Here,* Virgil Blossom insisted that he was in an impossible situation. The Bateses and other black Little Rockians wanted him to start integrating city schools immediately, while the all-white school board and many white parents opposed *any* kind of integration. During the summer of 1954 Blossom devised a schedule that he thought would be acceptable as a compromise. Little Rock schools would first integrate students in the lower grades. "It seemed to me that six-year-old children would be the least concerned about the color of the skin of classmates," he wrote. "They would not have had time to develop strong prejudices." Integration would gradually be expanded to the higher grades and would reach the high schools in a few years.

Hardly anyone liked Superintendent Blossom's original plan. It was just a delaying tactic, black leaders claimed. We need more time to prepare for integration, white parents and the school board insisted. Besides, they preferred to start with the oldest children—high school students—and then work down to the lower grades. Blossom, whose job depended on maintaining good relations with the school board, caved in and revamped his plan. Integration would begin three years later, in September 1957. It would start with a handful of high school students and proceed so slowly that the grade schools wouldn't be integrated until the 1960s. The Blossom Plan, as it became known, was approved by the Little Rock School Board and had repercussions far beyond the city. Seeing that their capital was implementing the Supreme Court's order at a snail's pace, other Arkansas cities such as North Little Rock, Hot Springs, and Fort Smith also decided to move slowly at integrating their schools.

Which Little Rock school would be integrated first? By 1957, the city would have four high schools: Horace Mann High, which was intended for black students; Hall and Central High Schools, which were intended for whites; and a technical high school that was also whites-only. Blossom and the school board decided to start by admitting a few black students to Central High, a massive structure two blocks long and five floors high, for the 1957–58 school year. Blossom privately boasted to friends that his plan would involve "the least amount of integration over the longest period."

Disgusted by the Blossom Plan, Daisy Bates consulted with national NAACP leaders about what to do. In the winter of 1955–56 she helped organize thirty-three black students of various ages who wanted to attend several all-white schools in Little Rock. The principals of all the schools refused to enroll the students, telling their families to discuss the matter with Mr. Blossom.

Daisy Bates arranged to visit the superintendent with nine pupils ranging in age from first grade to high school. Accompanied by the Reverend J. C. Crenchaw, president of the Little Rock branch of the NAACP, as well as a *State Press* photographer, Mrs. Bates and the nine young people arrived at Mr. Blossom's office at nine-thirty on a morning in early 1956. Virgil Blossom wrote, "Somebody also had notified the [area] newspapers of the attempt to enroll the Negro children and there was a battery of reporters and photographers on hand." That "somebody" was probably Daisy Bates, who expected Blossom to reject the black students' request and thought that newspaper pictures showing the children being turned away would gain sympathy for her cause.

After the crowd had been ushered into Mr. Blossom's office, Mrs. Bates said, "These children are here to enroll. They have already been to the various schools in which they want to enroll and the principals told them to come here. There is one child seeking to enroll in each grade level."

The superintendent remained firm. "No," he told Mrs. Bates and Reverend Crenchaw, "I cannot permit such registrations. We are going to follow the plan of gradual integration."

"Well, may we have a picture taken?" Daisy Bates asked. Mr. Blossom had no objection, and the photographers went to work.

The reporters then asked what Mrs. Bates planned to do next. "I think the next step is obvious," she replied. "We've tried everything short of a court suit."

On February 8, 1956, NAACP lawyer Wiley Branton, who had been one of the first black University of Arkansas graduates, filed a suit in federal court. It asserted that the Little Rock School Board had discriminated against the thirty-three black students by excluding them from the all-white schools.

In anticipation of the trial, Daisy Bates gave a deposition (pretrial testimony) on May 4, 1956. As the Arkansas NAACP president testified regarding the thirty-three students, one of the four school board attorneys repeatedly called her

"Daisy." A common way for white people to show disrespect for African Americans was to call them by their first names instead of "Mr.," "Miss," or "Mrs." When the afternoon session opened and the attorney again called her "Daisy," Mrs. Bates leaned forward in the witness chair. Staring at the attorney with contempt, she said, "You addressed me several times this morning by my first name. That is something reserved for my friends and my husband. You will refrain from calling me Daisy again."

Taken aback by the chastisement, the attorney muttered, "Well, I won't call you anything then."

The actual trial, which was held in August 1956, didn't go so well. The school board was acting with reasonable speed by starting integration the following year, ruled Federal Judge John E. Miller. The NAACP lawyers, including Thurgood Marshall and Wiley Branton, decided to appeal. The United States Court of Appeals in St. Louis, Missouri, heard the case in March of 1957. The court ruled that it was reasonable to begin integrating Little Rock's schools in September 1957.

Daisy Bates and the NAACP lawyers saw a silver lining in their court defeat. True, the appeals court had ruled that the Little Rock schools didn't have to integrate immediately or include all grades at once. However, the court had also said that integration should begin as planned in September 1957.

In a few months school integration would finally begin in the Arkansas capital— or so it appeared.

Daisy Bates and the Little Rock Nine. Seated (*from left*): Thelma Mothershed, Minnijean Brown, Elizabeth Eckford, Gloria Ray. Standing (*from left*): Terrance Roberts, Melba Pattillo, Jefferson Thomas, Carlotta Walls, Daisy Bates, and Ernest Green.

9

"Daisy, Daisy, Did You Hear the News?"

By the summer of 1957 Daisy Bates was known throughout Arkansas as the champion of school integration. Those who favored it viewed her as a heroine, while opponents considered her a troublemaker. Quite a few black people were wary of her. Having been oppressed for so many years, they feared that Mrs. Bates would only bring down more trouble on their heads.

Daisy Bates was so closely associated with school integration that many people assumed *she* handpicked the students who were selected to integrate Central High. Actually, they were chosen by Superintendent Virgil Blossom and other school officials.

First, Mr. Blossom asked the principals of the city's black junior and senior high schools to send him lists of pupils wanting to enroll at Central. They sent about eighty names—far more than Blossom and the school board wanted to start with. The superintendent then told the principals to weed out applicants who were not "mentally and emotionally equipped for this transition." By this method, the number of applicants was reduced from eighty to thirty-two.

Mr. Blossom then held individual conferences with the thirty-two remaining pupils and their families. Sitting with the students' records before him, Blossom convinced fifteen young people that Central High wasn't right for them for one reason or another. Seventeen remained. As the tension mounted in the weeks before school opened, seven more students backed out. That left ten youngsters to begin integrating Central High School, which had admitted only white students since opening in 1927.

Although she hadn't chosen the ten students, the Arkansas NAACP president began meeting with them at her home. They included students entering the last three years of high school: sophomore, junior, and senior years. The ten young people formed an impressive group:

- **Minnijean Brown** Sixteen-year-old Minnijean was a tall, friendly, multi-talented junior. She possessed a beautiful singing voice, enjoyed dancing, and was very athletic. Her main reason for transferring to Central, she explained, was that it was closer to home. "Central is only nine blocks away," she said, "and Horace Mann is a mile and a half if not two miles. I can easily walk to Central."

- **Elizabeth Eckford** A fifteen-year-old junior, Elizabeth wanted to enroll at Central for two reasons. She believed that Central's excellent academic reputation would help her toward her goal of becoming a lawyer. She also realized the historical importance of school integration. Her parents feared for her safety, but with difficulty she convinced them to let her attend Central.

- **Ernest Green** The only senior among the ten students, sixteen-year-old Ernest impressed everyone as mature beyond his years. Daisy Bates wrote about him: "Ernest possessed level judgment, and he never seemed to become ruffled. He always carried about him an air of calm assurance." Ernest had met a few white Central High students while working as a locker-room attendant at a country club, and he felt that this would help him win acceptance at school.

- **Jane Hill** A fifteen-year-old sophomore, Jane said that she wanted to attend Central because it offered more courses and was closer to home than Horace Mann. Her goal was to become a physician or an x-ray technician.

- **Thelma Mothershed** A sixteen-year-old junior, Thelma had a heart condition that made climbing stairs difficult and caused her to feel faint at times. Although her parents feared that attending Central would be too much of a strain for her, Thelma wanted to follow in the footsteps of her two older sisters: Lois, the first black student admitted to Phillips University in Enid, Oklahoma, and Grace, an early black member of the University of Arkansas nursing program. After failing to talk Thelma out of transferring to Central, her father said: "I was secretly pulling for her, and I was proud when she stood up to us."

• **Melba Pattillo** A fifteen-year-old junior, Melba sang, played the piano, and loved rock and roll music. She was bitterly disappointed when she couldn't attend a 1956 Elvis Presley concert in Little Rock because blacks weren't admitted. Melba hoped to become an actress or singer. "When my teacher asked if anyone who lived within the Central High School district wanted to attend school with white people, I raised my hand," Melba explained. She didn't tell her parents, who found out about it after she was mentioned on the news as a candidate to integrate Central High.

• **Gloria Ray** A fifteen-year-old junior who dreamed of becoming an atomic scientist, Gloria informed her mother that she intended to enroll at Central High. However, they both kept it secret from her father, a man in his sixties with a heart condition. Only after his daughter had entered Central High did Mr. Ray realize that his "baby" was not attending Horace Mann High School as he had believed. Daisy Bates helped convince Mr. Ray that he shouldn't stop his daughter from attending Central.

• **Terrance Roberts** A fifteen-year-old junior, Terrance was one of the most scholarly of the ten students. Melba, who had been his friend since first grade, described him as "a very verbal person who could be counted on to give the funniest, most intelligent analysis of any situation. I adored his way of always humming a cheerful tune when he wasn't talking." Like Jane Hill, Terrance wanted to become a doctor.

• **Jefferson Thomas** Unlike the talkative Terrance, fifteen-year-old Jefferson Thomas was quiet and soft-spoken. At his all-black junior high Jefferson had been a track star and student council president. Since the Little Rock School Board had decided that the black students at Central couldn't take part in sports or student government, he knew he would have to forsake these activities. A sophomore, Jefferson had dreamed of becoming a great architect since the age of ten.

- **Carlotta Walls** The youngest of the ten students, fourteen-year-old Carlotta was a tall, athletic sophomore who enjoyed swimming and bowling. She was also one of the most talented baseball players in her neighborhood, which was one of the few integrated sections of Little Rock. "I've played with all my neighbors both black and white as long as I can remember," she explained, so, like Ernest Green, she didn't expect the white students at Central to treat her badly.

While recognizing the importance of what their sons and daughters were doing, the ten students' families were worried about them. Hosana Mothershed, Thelma's mother, said that in a way she "wanted her to go to Central and in another way I didn't." On the one hand, she explained, "I kept thinking about her weak heart." But on the other hand, she knew that it was "up to Thelma to pave the way for [her two younger brothers] and all the other Negro kids who would come behind her. If she goes to school there now, then it will be easier for the others coming along." Probably the staunchest supporter of his child was Cartelyou Walls, Carlotta's father. "She has a right to go there," said Mr. Walls, a World War II veteran who had won at least three awards for bravery in action. "My tax money is not separated from the rest of the tax money. There is no reason for her to pass one school to go to another [farther from home]."

As she met with the students near the opening of school in 1957, Daisy Bates agreed with Virgil Blossom on one matter. That May Mr. Blossom had told NAACP leaders that the black students at Central should model themselves after Jackie Robinson. A decade earlier, in 1947, Robinson had become modern major league baseball's first black player. Selected to break baseball's color barrier partly because of his fine personal character, Robinson had shown remarkable restraint in ignoring racial slurs hurled at him by fans and fellow ballplayers, including some of his own teammates. Over time his dignified manner and exciting style of play had won the respect of fans and players, paving the way for other black major leaguers. Elizabeth Eckford, who spoke to us in Little Rock in early 2003, related that sometime around the beginning of school in 1957, Daisy Bates arranged for a minister from Nashville, Tennessee, to come and "give us lessons on nonviolence." Mrs. Bates hoped that because they were such fine young people and serious students, the ten black children would gradually win acceptance, much like Jackie Robinson.

That might have happened if not for some adults.

As Daisy Bates was counseling the students, the bigots were mobilizing to oppose school integration. Prejudice against blacks was the main but not the only reason. Since the 1800s white southerners had argued for "states' rights"—the idea that in many local matters individual states, not the federal government, should have the final say. One major reason for the Civil War was that President Abraham Lincoln opposed slavery, an issue southern whites wanted each state to decide for itself. Now, almost a century later, states' righters argued that the U.S. Supreme Court had no right to tell them when and how to integrate their schools. Of course, if the states' righters had their way, slavery would have still existed in 1957 and school integration would never have occurred.

The segregationists formed groups to fight integration. A group in Little Rock, the Capital Citizens' Council, was led by attorney Amis Guthridge. Another, the Mothers' League of Central High School, was composed of mothers of white students. These and other racist groups passed out leaflets, spoke to newspapers, and held rallies. A favorite tactic of theirs was to claim that Communism—the system of government in the Soviet Union—was behind the effort to integrate Central High. W. R. Hughes, a Texan who spoke to the Mothers' League, declared that Communism was "behind every effort of the NAACP." Mr. Hughes also warned the women: "A nigger in your school is a potential Communist in your school. Stand up and fight for your children and never cease as long as you can breathe." Another man stood up at a Mothers' League meeting and demanded to know how many people would come to Central High to "push back" black children trying to enter. "And I imagine there are a few shotguns in Little Rock, too!" he added.

The white students, many of whose parents belonged to these groups, were influenced by all the racist talk they heard. Worse yet, most southern lawmakers sided with the segregationists.

In 1956 southern lawmakers issued the Southern Manifesto, which pledged its signers to fight the 1954 Supreme Court school integration order. About 85 percent of the representatives and senators from the southern states signed the document. Every Arkansas representative, and both of the state's U.S. senators, John L. McClellan and J. William Fulbright, signed the Southern Manifesto. Fulbright's action devastated many people who expected him to oppose the document. Had he not signed, he explained, he wouldn't have been reelected to the Senate. Daisy Bates told the *Afro-American* newspaper of Baltimore that she was especially disgusted with politicians who sided with blacks "behind closed doors" but then went along with the racists when the chips were down.

Another important lawmaker was yet to be heard from, and there was reason to think he would support school integration. Arkansas governor Orval E. Faubus had been taught about the evils of racism while growing up in his backwoods home in northwestern Arkansas. His father, an organizer for the Socialist party, had sent him briefly to a school with Communist ties, Commonwealth College in Mena, Arkansas. In 1954, when Faubus first ran for his state's highest office, then-governor Francis Cherry tried to smear him for his family's Socialist and Communist leanings. Faubus went on TV to say he was the victim of unfair tactics. Yes, he admitted, he had attended Commonwealth, but he had been young and poor and had needed the scholarship. Besides, he hadn't known anything about the college. His appeal for fair play worked, and he was elected, taking office as governor in 1955.

By 1957 Faubus was in his second term as governor and was proud of his record on racial issues. Under Faubus a number of African Americans were appointed to state office, and by 1957 Arkansas had desegregated more schools than eleven other southern states combined. Racist opponents accused him of

Mrs. Bates holds empty cartridges and a letter warning her to leave town or die.

sympathizing with or even belonging to the NAACP. Like many other people, Daisy Bates hoped that, given his background, Faubus would support or at least not oppose integration at Central High. But as the opening of school approached, the governor's position was not yet clear.

Serious trouble erupted as summer vacation ended.

On Thursday, August 22, the rock came crashing through the Bateses' picture window. L.C. had a permit to carry a loaded revolver. He, Daisy, and several friends, including their next-door neighbor, a dentist named Garman Freeman, began taking turns guarding the Bates home at night. By this time Daisy Bates was receiving so many threats by phone and letter that, for protection, she placed a loaded gun in her car's glove compartment.

On Tuesday, August 27, Mrs. Clyde A. Thomason, Mothers' League recording secretary, filed a suit seeking a temporary injunction—a court order—preventing the integration of Central High.

On Thursday, August 29, a Pulaski County judge, Murray O. Reed, heard Mrs. Thomason's suit. The first witness, Mrs. Thomason herself, testified that people she wouldn't identify had told her "in strict confidence" that there would be violence if Central High opened as an integrated school the following Tuesday. Rumors were flying that "two gangs are forming, one of white boys and the other colored boys," and that one of the gangs had knives and guns. "The mothers are terrified," she said, "and are afraid to send their children to Central High School."

Another witness, Marvin Potts, refuted Mrs. Thomason, insisting there was no evidence that white and black gangs intended to disrupt school. His testimony should have carried great weight, for Potts was Little Rock's police chief. Superintendent Virgil Blossom and Dr. William Cooper Jr., a surgeon who was president of the Little Rock School Board, also testified that they expected no violence.

Governor Orval Faubus (*left*) and Superintendent Virgil Blossom.

But a surprise witness supported Mrs. Thomason's claims. Governor Orval Faubus walked into the courtroom and testified that he personally knew of cases in which guns had been seized from black and white students. Until a month earlier, he added, he had believed that Little Rockians, although opposed to integration, would peacefully obey the Supreme Court's integration order. Now he didn't think so, especially after Georgia governor Marvin Griffin's inflammatory speech a week earlier. In fact, this was a terrible time to integrate Central High, Faubus now believed. "A crowd can assemble with the best intentions," he said, "and become a mob just because of two or three hotheaded people."

Largely because of the governor's testimony, Judge Reed ruled in Mrs. Thomason's favor. "I feel," said the judge, "that I can only rule to grant the injunction against starting integration."

Daisy Bates was deeply disappointed. As governor, Faubus could have declared that the Supreme Court's school integration order must be obeyed and that violence wouldn't be tolerated. Instead, he was hiding behind rumors of violence to prevent integration. Worse yet, by stirring up angry feelings, he was making trouble more likely. Faubus apparently had decided to do what would make him more popular rather than what he knew was right.

At that time Arkansas was home to about 1.8 million people. Whites comprised about 78 percent of the population, blacks 22 percent, and all other races less than 1 percent. According to a poll the vast majority of white Arkansans opposed integration. Faubus hoped to win a third term as governor in 1958, and supporting integration might cost him the election.

The racists celebrated Judge Reed's decision. On the night of August 29, people drove past the Bates home, honking their horns and shouting: "Daisy, Daisy, did you hear the news? The coons won't be going to Central!"

But the next day, Friday, August 30, NAACP attorneys Wiley Branton and Thurgood Marshall went before the U.S. District Court asking to have Judge Reed's order overruled. The case was heard by Judge Ronald Davies, who had recently been appointed to fill a vacancy. The integration of Central High must proceed as planned, Judge Davies ruled. Furthermore, he issued an order that no one interfere with the black students entering the school. Judge Davies "just did not understand the problem," complained Mrs. Thomason, referring to the fact that he was from North Dakota and was more interested in the law than in local customs.

By August 30, Arkansas officials had begun trying to intimidate Daisy Bates. That day Arkansas Attorney General Bruce Bennett sent her a letter demanding that she answer fourteen questions relating to the Arkansas NAACP's operations, membership, and finances. For example, she must "list the names and addresses of the officers which make up the various local branches of the Arkansas NAACP." Bennett hoped to destroy the Arkansas NAACP by threatening to prosecute its leaders under some technicality.

Mrs. Bates refused to answer his questions. The harassment continued for more than two years, until the U.S. Supreme Court ruled that such demands "violate freedom of speech and assembly guaranteed by the First Amendment."

On Labor Day, September 2, 1957, Jefferson Thomas stopped by the Bates home for a visit. School was to begin the next morning, and he wanted to talk to Mrs. Bates. He was fixing himself a snack when a news flash came over the radio. Governor Faubus planned to speak to Arkansas citizens that night.

"I wonder what he's going to talk about," Jefferson said to Mrs. Bates. "Is there anything they can do now that they lost in court? Is there any way they can stop us from entering Central tomorrow morning?"

"I don't think so," Daisy Bates reassured him.

But that night at nine o'clock, 300 Arkansas National Guardsmen began to surround Central High. Governor Faubus had called these emergency troops to active duty—why was not yet known. At ten-fifteen P.M. the governor spoke on local TV and radio. He was vague about his reasons for calling out the Arkansas National Guard while claiming that "they will act not as segregationists or integrationists, but as soldiers" there to keep the peace.

Then he revealed which side he had taken. "It is my opinion that it will not be possible to restore or to maintain order and protect the lives and property of the citizens if forcible integration is carried out tomorrow. The schools, for the time being, must be

operated on the same basis as they have in the past." In other words, for an unspeci-
fied period the ten black students must stay out of Central High.

Classes at Central began at eight-forty-five A.M. on Tuesday, September 3. The
National Guardsmen, as well as a crowd of 400 white adults, watched as nearly
2,000 students, none of them black, entered the school. The only black person at
the scene was L.C. Bates, who came as a reporter. At one point a group of out-of-
town racists rushed toward L.C., probably to try to beat him up. Suddenly, he
reached into his pocket. Local whites warned the out-of-towners that Bates had a
permit to carry a loaded gun, and the thugs backed off. When asked by visiting
white newsmen how he had summoned the nerve to face the mob, L.C. quipped:
"I just came by to add some color to the occasion."

Meanwhile, Superintendent Blossom and the school board were uncertain
about what they should do, so they asked Federal Judge Ronald Davies for instructions. Daisy Bates and Carlotta
Walls were in the courtroom when
Judge Davies announced his decision on the evening of September 3.
The judge said that Governor
Faubus should be taken at his
word: The Guardsmen were not
acting as segregationists or integrationists but were there to keep the
peace. The black students would
enter Central High the next day,
September 4.

Daisy Bates hurried home to
prepare for what she expected to be
the most important day of her life.

Judge Ronald Davies signing his ruling that
Central High School must integrate.

Fifteen-year-old Elizabeth Eckford endures insults from a white mob outside Central High School on September 4, 1957.

10

"They're In!"

L.C. hadn't gone to Central High on September 3 just to report on the start of school for the *State Press.* He had wanted to see the size and mood of the crowd. When Daisy Bates heard that there had been 400 people, including some who had arrived in cars with out-of-state license plates, she was worried. If 400 people gathered when *no* black students were scheduled to arrive, how many might show up the next morning? When L.C. told her about the thugs who had been about to rush him, her worries grew.

People went in and out of the Bates house that night asking what she thought would happen and what she planned to do. One of them was the Reverend J. C. Crenchaw, president of the Little Rock NAACP branch. Seeing Reverend Crenchaw gave her an idea.

"Maybe," she said, "we could round up a few ministers to go with the children tomorrow. Maybe then the mob won't attack them."

Mrs. Bates phoned the Reverend Dunbar Ogden Jr., one of Little Rock's few white clergymen who favored school integration. President of an organization called the Interracial Ministerial Alliance, Reverend Ogden said he would contact some ministers and then call her back.

When the phone rang, Daisy Bates could hear the disappointment in Reverend Ogden's voice. The black ministers had said that Superintendent

Blossom had asked them to stay away from the school because their presence might inflame the bigots. The white ministers had made various excuses. "I'll keep trying," said Reverend Ogden, "and, God willing, I'll be there." They agreed that the students, Mrs. Bates, Reverend Ogden, and any other clergymen he could convince would meet at eight-thirty A.M. at Twelfth and Park Streets.

Next she phoned the Little Rock Police to request that a squad car be stationed at Twelfth and Park before eight-thirty the next morning to protect the black students. Yes, they promised, but they could not escort the children all the way to Central.

It was two-thirty A.M. and Daisy Bates was exhausted. She still had to inform the ten students that they would gather at Twelfth and Park at eight-thirty and proceed as a group. It took her until three A.M. to complete those phone calls. However, she wasn't able to reach the home of Elizabeth Eckford, whose family didn't have a telephone. Mrs. Bates considered going to the railroad station, where she thought Elizabeth's father worked nights, but she was so tired that she decided to sleep a few hours and contact Elizabeth in the morning.

When she awoke, Daisy Bates called the NAACP's New York headquarters, which had been providing her with legal advice and moral support. Some of her conversations with the NAACP were taped, including this one on the morning of September 4 between Mrs. Bates and NAACP official Mr. Gloster Current:

> *DAISY BATES: We are getting ready to go to school. They have guards out there and there is a whole crowd of people out there now. We don't know for sure whether they will be admitted this morning.*
>
> *GLOSTER CURRENT: We understand from the newspapers this morning the judge ordered the school to go ahead [and integrate].*
>
> *DAISY BATES: Yes, last night it took him about thirty seconds to do it. If the children are denied admittance this morning, the responsibility will rest on the governor. I haven't slept two hours. It's now ten minutes to eight here. If the children are admitted I will call you and if they are not admitted I will call you. We will have to do something and do it quickly.*

GLOSTER CURRENT: *Well, keep your chin up.*

DAISY BATES: *We should know in about thirty minutes.*

Daisy and L.C. got into their car and began driving toward Twelfth and Park. On the way they switched on the radio and heard a news bulletin: "A Negro girl is being mobbed at Central High. . . ."

"Oh, my God!" Daisy Bates cried in horror. She had forgotten to notify Elizabeth that they were meeting and driving to school together.

L.C. scrambled out of the car and ran toward the high school to find out about Elizabeth. Furious at herself for neglecting something so important, Daisy Bates drove on to the meeting place. Reverend Ogden was there with his twenty-one-year-old son, David Ogden, as well as another white minister, the Reverend Will Campbell, and two black ministers, the Reverend Z. Z. Driver and the Reverend Harry Bass. As promised, a police car was there, and all the students had arrived except Elizabeth. The three or four cars containing the students and the adults accompanying them parked near the high school.

Meanwhile, Elizabeth Eckford, unaware of the plan, had taken a bus to school. Wearing a black-and-white dress she had made for her first day of classes, and carrying a green notebook, Elizabeth stepped off the bus at about eight A.M. and began walking the final block to Central High. Outside the school she saw a line of armed Guardsmen and a crowd of some 400 white people. At first Elizabeth was glad to see the National Guardsmen and assumed they were there to protect her. But whenever she tried to get past them to enter the school, the guards blocked her path, even raising their bayonets to keep her away. At the same time, the Guardsmen allowed the white students through. Noticing that the lone black student was trying to get into the school, the crowd closed in on her, yelling "Lynch her!" and "Go home, black bitch!"

For a few moments she stood trembling as she looked at the crowd through her sunglasses. Elizabeth later recalled: "I tried to see a friendly face somewhere in the mob—somebody who maybe would help. I looked into the face of an old woman, but when I looked at her again, she spat on me."

79

Not knowing what else to do, Elizabeth began walking toward the bus stop down the block. The crowd, still shouting threats, followed her, as did several newsmen and photographers. After what seemed like an eternity, Elizabeth sat down on a bench by the bus stop and began crying. As the tears streaked down Elizabeth's cheeks, *New York Times* education editor Benjamin Fine sat next to her. Dr. Fine put his arm around Elizabeth, raised her chin, and said, "Don't let them see you cry." Several other people, including a white woman named Grace Lorch and L.C. Bates, also approached Elizabeth to comfort and protect her.

Elizabeth Eckford seeks refuge at the bus stop.

Apparently, the mob figured it was natural for Mr. Bates to aid one of his own people, for they let him alone, but they hurled insults at Mrs. Lorch and Dr. Fine. "Nigger lover!" the mob shouted at Mrs. Lorch. "Dirty Jew!" someone screamed at Dr. Fine. After a few minutes a bus came and Elizabeth boarded it, leaving the ugly mob behind.

L.C. ran back to the little caravan of cars that was waiting near the school and described Elizabeth's ordeal to his wife. The nine other students stepped out of the cars. With two ministers leading the way and two bringing up the rear, the students began walking toward Central High in a line. The racists hated Mrs. Bates so intensely that her presence at the school might have sparked a riot, so she and several others who had come along remained in the cars.

As the students approached, the mob closed in on them. There was some pushing and shoving, but Daisy Bates's idea to have the ministers accompany them worked, for none of the youngsters was attacked. Before the black students could enter the building, however, the troops on guard motioned them to halt. Lieutenant Colonel Marion Johnson, who commanded the Guardsmen at Central High, came to speak to the black students and the ministers.

The Reverend Harry Bass asked Lieutenant Colonel Johnson if the Guardsmen were preventing the children from entering the school. That was correct, Johnson answered. Reverend Bass persisted: "I just want to get this straight. You are doing this on the orders of the governor, is that correct?"

"That is right," answered the lieutenant colonel.

"All right," Reverend Bass said, "we do not want to disobey any orders of the governor, so we will leave."

The ministers and the students returned to the cars and told Daisy Bates what had happened. She took the students to speak to Superintendent Blossom, but he was out and did not return during the next hour. Later in the day Mrs. Bates took the students to the Little Rock office of the Federal Bureau of Investigation. There the students gave a detailed account of what had occurred at the school that morning.

By now it was apparent that Governor Faubus had been lying. He had stationed the National Guard at Central High to keep the black students out, as

The September 6, 1957, front page of L.C. and Daisy Bates's newspaper.

Lieutenant Colonel Marion Johnson had admitted. Soon the whole nation knew what had happened, for TV crews, reporters, and photographers had recorded the day's events. In fact, over the next few months the Little Rock school crisis became one of the first ongoing news stories covered by on-site television crews.

Following the tense events of September 4, 1957, Jane Hill decided to attend all-black Horace Mann High School. The remaining African American students who wanted to enter Central High were given a nickname by which they became known to the world: "the Little Rock Nine."

With the National Guardsmen continuing to surround the school, the Little Rock Nine had to stay out. Nearly three weeks passed and still they couldn't enter. During that time the president of the United States, Dwight D. Eisenhower, exchanged telegrams with Governor Faubus. The president was furious at the Arkansas governor's actions. Governor Faubus had defied the U.S. Supreme

Court's order to integrate the schools and Federal Judge Ronald Davies's order that Central High begin integration on September 4. He had turned the phrase "with liberty and justice for all," recited by millions of American schoolchildren each morning, into hollow words. He had helped convince people around the world who were watching events unfold in Little Rock that Americans were bigoted and cruel. The president, who was nicknamed "Ike," was so angry that there was talk he might have the Arkansas governor arrested. The September 5 *Arkansas Democrat* carried a story headlined: "IKE DENIES FAUBUS ARREST UNDER STUDY."

The president tried to convince the Arkansas governor to change his mind and admit the black students. On September 14 Faubus flew to Newport, Rhode Island, to meet with the president at one of Ike's favorite golfing retreats. During their

President Dwight D. Eisenhower.

two-hour-and-ten-minute conference, Faubus proposed that the integration of Little Rock schools be delayed for a year-long "cooling-off period." President Eisenhower rejected the proposal. Six days later Judge Davies held another hearing on the school crisis and ordered that Governor Faubus stop interfering with the integration of Central High. Realizing that he might be sent to jail if he continued to block integration, Faubus removed the Arkansas National Guard troops from their positions around the school. He then flew off to attend the Southern Governors' Conference at Sea Island, Georgia.

Meanwhile, the Little Rock Nine were meeting with NAACP officials and other civil rights leaders at Daisy Bates's home. They kept up their education by studying with professors at Philander Smith College, a school for African Americans in Little Rock. To escape the reporters who were flocking to her home to interview her, Elizabeth Eckford stayed with the Bateses for a few days in September. Elizabeth suffered recurrent nightmares about facing the mob alone. Over the next few weeks Elizabeth remained depressed and silent whenever the Nine gathered to talk. She seemed to perk up only when NAACP attorney Thurgood Marshall came to explain the importance of what they were doing.

The first time Mrs. Bates asked her how she felt about what had happened, Elizabeth glared at her and snapped: "Why are you so interested in my welfare *now?* You didn't care enough to notify me of the change of plans!" Realizing that nothing she could say would excuse what she had done, Daisy Bates vowed to herself that she would not make a similar mistake again.

One afternoon shortly after the events of September 4, a middle-aged white woman came to her house to talk to Mrs. Bates. She said she represented a group of "southern Christian women," which may have been the Mothers' League of Central High School. Her organization, said the woman, wanted Daisy Bates to use her influence to convince the black students to withdraw their applications to attend Central. "This will give us time to prepare the community for integration," she told Mrs. Bates.

"How much time?" Daisy Bates asked. The woman wasn't sure but repeated that Mrs. Bates should call a press conference and announce that she was asking the students to return to the black schools "for the good of the community." Daisy Bates would be criticized up north for doing this, the woman said, but she needn't worry because the "southern Christian women" would support her decision.

After listening for an hour, Mrs. Bates said: "You told me what would happen if I withdraw my support from the students. What will happen if I don't?"

Instantly, the woman's friendly tone vanished. "You'll be destroyed," she told Mrs. Bates. "You, your newspaper, your reputation—*everything!*" Before departing, the woman gave Daisy Bates her phone number and said she expected an answer by nine the next morning.

The threats were not idle chatter, Daisy Bates knew. These people could seriously hurt the *State Press* by pressuring businesses to withdraw their advertisements. They were also capable of violence—as the broken picture window proved.

At two A.M., Daisy Bates was thinking about what she would say the next morning when she heard a muffled cry. Entering the bedroom where Elizabeth was sleeping, she found her thrashing about from a nightmare. She spoke gently to Elizabeth until she calmed down and went back to sleep.

Mrs. Bates then went into her living room. Staring out the picture window, now held together with masking tape, she noticed a car cruising by. The volunteer guard standing outside the house raised his gun. Suddenly, there was a loud explosion. She thought it was a bomb before realizing that someone in the car had thrown a firecracker.

Daisy Bates was shaken and angry—perhaps angrier than she had ever been since her childhood. She walked to a table and picked up a small china vase that had been her most treasured possession since her adoptive grandmother in New Edinburg had given it to her for her fifth birthday. The vase had been handed down in their family from slavery days, possibly bought with the pennies slaves sometimes received for doing extra chores, her grandmother had explained. "Somehow, to me it represented my roots, my family, their appreciation for beauty at a time when they were subjected to brutality and degradation," Daisy wrote.

For reasons she never could explain, she suddenly threw the vase against the fireplace, smashing it to pieces. Seven hours later, at nine A.M., she phoned the woman. Her answer was *no,* Daisy Bates said, adding that the woman and her friends were just bigots hiding behind the name of Christianity. Daisy Bates then went to the *State Press* office and wrote an article about the episode.

"Daisy, you did the right thing," L.C. assured her, even after businesses began to withdraw their advertisements from the *State Press.*

September 20—the day Judge Davies ordered Governor Faubus to stop interfering with school integration—was a Friday. The black students would again attempt to enter Central High on Monday, September 23. Late Sunday night Superintendent Blossom phoned Mrs. Bates. He thought it best for the Nine to meet at her home on Monday morning and await instructions on how to proceed to school. Daisy Bates asked how the students would be protected and was told that the Little Rock police under Assistant Chief Gene Smith would now be responsible for keeping order at

This 1957 cartoon from the *Afro-American* of Baltimore, Maryland, attacks Governor Faubus's use of the National Guard to bar black students from Central High.

Central High. This time Mrs. Bates made sure that all of the nine students knew about the plan.

The students and their parents arrived at the Bates home at about eight A.M. on Monday. By then a number of journalists—black and white—had made the Bates house their headquarters. They included Alex Wilson, editor of the *Tri-State Defender* of Memphis, Tennessee; Earl Davy, photographer for the *Arkansas State Press;* and other newspapermen from as far away as New York and Baltimore. All over the Bates house the students, their parents, and the journalists were listening to radio interviews of people gathering outside Central High. One man interviewed on the sidewalk warned: "Just let those niggers show up! Let 'em try!" Another member of the crowd proclaimed: "We won't stand for our schools being integrated."

The students were frightened yet determined to attend school that morning. Carlotta Walls and Ernest Green were pacing nervously around the house. Elizabeth sat by herself, barely moving a muscle. Her father, Oscar Eckford, and Minnijean's mother, Imogene Brown, were silently praying.

At a few minutes after eight the police phoned Daisy Bates and told her to take the Nine by a roundabout route to a certain spot near Central High. The police promised to meet the Nine, then escort them through a side entrance.

They went in two cars. Daisy and some of the students rode in one car with Christopher Mercer, a local African American attorney. NAACP official Frank Smith drove the other car containing the rest of the Nine. The reporters and photographers who had camped at the Bates house headed to the school by a separate route.

The two cars with the nine students went to the assigned spot. The police met the Nine there and quickly whisked them through a side entrance. At first the mob, which numbered more than a thousand people, didn't realize that the students had entered the school.

Then someone inside the school called to the crowd through an open window: "They're in!"

Integration had begun at Central High.

Soldiers from the famous 101st Airborne Division of the U.S. Army escort five of the Little Rock Nine from Central High School during the 1957 crisis.

11

"Some Victory!"

Standing next to her car, Daisy Bates watched the students enter the school. She then noticed people along the edge of the crowd moving toward the two cars that had brought the students. A policeman ran up and said, "Get back in the car, Mrs. Bates! Drive back the way you came—and fast!"

As she and Mr. Mercer sped off, they switched on the car radio. "The Negro children are being mobbed in front of the school," an announcer said. This wasn't true, Mrs. Bates knew, for she had just seen the students go in by the side entrance. Whom was the mob attacking in front of the school?

Five minutes before the Nine entered Central High, several black newspapermen had arrived at the front of the school to obtain stories and pictures of the mob scene. Screaming, "Get the niggers!" part of the mob rushed them. They kicked and punched *State Press* photographer Earl Davy and New York's *Amsterdam News* managing editor James Hicks, but Memphis *Tri-State Defender* editor Alex Wilson became their main target.

Several white men jumped on Wilson, throwing him to the ground and kicking and punching him. As Wilson got up, one of his attackers yelled, "Run, nigger!" But Wilson, who had served as a U.S. Marine in World War II, refused to run. He later said that "the vision of Elizabeth Eckford flashed before me as she with dignity strode through the jeering, hooting segregationists several days ago."

Reporter Alex Wilson is mobbed, jumped, . . .

Wilson's refusal to run enraged his attackers, one of whom struck him on the head with a brick. Suddenly there were yells of "The niggers are in the school!" and the mob turned away from the injured black newspapermen, who later returned to Daisy Bates's home and told her what had occurred.

Realizing that the Nine were already inside Central High, a portion of the mob fanned out toward where Daisy Bates was standing. Members of the crowd that had remained in front of the building began shouting for their sons and daughters to leave school. Approximately fifty white students ran outside, some to protest integration, others out of fear that there might be a bomb or rioting in the school.

Meanwhile, a student council officer had met the Nine and led them through the hallway. The strain had been too much for Thelma Mothershed. Once inside Principal Jess Matthews's office, she slumped to the floor, struggling for breath.

Assistant Principal Elizabeth Huckaby sent for the nurse to aid Thelma. Soon after, staff members took all of the Nine except Thelma to their classes. Once she felt better, Thelma headed to class too. But the staff was having difficulty keeping order in the school. White students in the corridors stood staring at the Nine and debating whether or not to walk out. Parents entered the school and asked to take their sons and daughters home.

Most of the students in the classrooms minded their own business that day, but some caused trouble. "Are you gonna let that nigger coon sit in our class?" a boy asked a teacher in front of Melba Pattillo. Others of the Nine were shoved, slapped, and chased through the hallways.

Outside, the crowd was growing more belligerent. "Two, four, six, eight, we ain't gonna integrate!" they chanted. Fights broke out between demonstrators and

. . . and kicked as he falls.

police. By about eleven A.M. Assistant Police Chief Gene Smith doubted that he could continue to control the mob. Smith, Little Rock Mayor Woodrow Mann, and Superintendent Virgil Blossom decided that the black students must leave the school for their own safety. At eleven-thirty the police took them out of the enormous building through a back delivery entrance. The Nine were hurried into police cars and driven to their homes.

The crowd didn't believe the police announcement that the black students were gone, so one woman was allowed to go inside and look around. When she reported that the Nine had departed, the crowd began to drift away. But some still thirsted for blood. Two black women driving near Central High were pulled from their car and beaten. Two black men were also attacked and had their truck's windows smashed. In addition, three *Life* magazine staff members were assaulted; then *they* were arrested for inciting a riot. Following their release, one of the three, photographer Francis Miller, commented that he had been arrested for attacking a man's fist with his face.

By that afternoon reporters were pouring into the Bates home to ask whether the Nine would return to Central or transfer to all-black Horace Mann High School. If the Nine left Central, Daisy Bates knew, the racists would view it as a triumph and integration might be delayed for years. The Nine would return to Central, she declared, insisting that it was President Eisenhower's duty to see that they were protected.

That night the violence continued as carloads of hoodlums drove through Little Rock, throwing bricks and bottles through the windows of black people's businesses and homes. Despite the vicious attack he had endured that morning, Alex Wilson helped L.C. and Garman Freeman stand guard at the Bates home all night. Around midnight a police officer came by the house to warn that a motorcade of dozens of cars had been stopped nearby. The police had searched the cars and had found guns and dynamite. At about two-thirty A.M. the phone rang. Daisy Bates answered and heard a man's voice say, "We didn't get you last night, but we will!" The Bateses couldn't sleep at all that night—a situation that would be repeated many times over the next few months.

The next day—Tuesday, September 24—the Nine stayed home from school. That afternoon Daisy Bates spoke to Gloster Current at the NAACP's New York headquarters. She wanted to make sure that the national NAACP leaders thought she was handling the situation properly. "Have you heard any of the statements I have made?" she asked Mr. Current.

"Everything you have said so far has been right on the button!" he reassured her.

At six-thirty that evening the Nine came to the Bates house for a meeting. They must return to Central as soon as it was safe, Daisy Bates told them. Then at seven they all watched President Eisenhower address the nation on TV. "My fellow citizens," said the president, "for a few minutes I want to speak to you about the situation that has arisen in Little Rock. In that city, under the leadership of extremists, disorderly mobs have deliberately prevented the carrying out of orders from a federal court. As you know, the Supreme Court of the United States has decided that separate public educational facilities are inherently unequal and therefore school segregation laws are unconstitutional." He was sending federal troops to Little Rock to make sure the law of the land was obeyed, the president explained.

Several hours before the president spoke, the troops had begun arriving at Little Rock Air Force Base outside the city. Fifty-two planeloads containing 1,200 paratroopers from the famed 101st Airborne Division landed at the air base. By nightfall the paratroopers were taking up positions at Central High. In addition, President Eisenhower "federalized" the Arkansas National Guard. This meant that many of the same Guardsmen who had previously been stationed at the school by Governor Faubus were returning there—only now they were to follow the president's order to protect the black students rather than keep them out.

A few minutes after midnight Mr. Blossom phoned Daisy Bates and told her that the Nine should be at her house by eight-thirty A.M. so that the federal troops could meet them and escort them to school. It was too late for Mrs. Bates to call the students: They had received so many threatening calls at odd hours that their families had begun leaving their telephones off the hook after midnight. Daisy Bates arranged for two black school principals to accompany her, and set off with

White students outside Central High School, September 1957; note the Army vehicles in the background.

them at one A.M. to visit the nine students' homes. Not until past four A.M. did Mrs. Bates and her companions finish notifying all the students' families about the plan.

The Nine were all at the Bates house by about eight-thirty A.M. Jefferson Thomas, standing by the window, was the first to see the military vehicles approaching. "The Army's here!" he called. "They're here!" Looking out the window, Minnijean Brown said, "Oh, look at them, they're so soldierly! It gives you goose pimples to look at them!" Melba Pattillo noticed that her mother and many of the other adults gathered at the house were crying. Minnijean Brown said what many of them were thinking: "For the first time in my life, I feel like an American citizen."

An officer came to the door and, when Daisy Bates opened it, saluted and announced: "Mrs. Bates, we're ready for the children. We will return them to your home at three-thirty o'clock."

The Nine were led into an Army station wagon. As they were driven to school, they were joined by a growing number of Army jeeps. Near the school an Army helicopter circled overhead. Soldiers were clearing away the crowd, which was chanting, "Two, four, six, eight, we ain't gonna integrate!" In her autobiography, *Warriors Don't Cry,* Melba Pattillo Beals later recalled:

> Closer to the school, we saw more soldiers and many more hostile white people with scowls on their faces, lining the sidewalk and shaking their fists. But for the first time I wasn't afraid of them. . . . I felt proud and sad at the same time. Proud that I lived in a country that would go this far to bring justice to a Little Rock girl like me, but sad that they had to go to such great lengths. . . . I walked on the concrete path toward the front door of the school, the same path the Arkansas National Guard had blocked us from days before.

At nine twenty-two A.M.—about half an hour late—the Nine entered Central High. Soldiers were inside the building too. Each of the Nine was assigned to a soldier, who escorted him or her from class to class.

95

9:25 A.M., Thurs., Sept. 25, 1957

Time And Date Of Historic Action

By BOB CONSIDINE

LITTLE ROCK, Ark. — (INS) — Tough, determined federal troops shepherded nine Negro students into Little Rocks Central High school today and engaged in a series of skirmishes with protesting segregationists which injured two white men.

One of them was conked in the head with a rifle butt and the other was bayonetted in the right arm, apparently accidentally, but otherwise little blood flowed.

The six girls and three boys arrived at the high school in an Army station wagon which had picked them up at Mrs. L. C. Bates home. Flanked by a platoon of GI's, they entered the building at 9:25 a. m. (CST)

BATTLE FAME

Thus did the 101st Airborne Division, which gained eternal fame during the Battle of the Bulge in World War II, carry out President Eisenhower's order to enforce a federal court decision that Central High must be integrated.

Several blocks away from the big, tense, partly depopulated school where the nine Negro

dents. An estimated 700 of the 2,000 pupils remained away from their desks.

Less than a minute after the nine Negroes entered the school, one white boy emerged from the building, walked down the steps in lonely grandeur, and disappeared from the heavily-guarded scene.

There was a thin, ragged cheer for him from the crowd that showed up near the school and was kept under strict control by the troops from the division of Bastogne fame.

The Negro students, all A-scholars, were picked up from their several homes in an army station wagon. They appeared completely unfrightened as they spilled out of the vehicle at a wooden barricade erected to kep traffic off the street in front of the school.

HISTORIC EVENT

The bayonetted-bristling platoon quickly formed a protective screen around the Negroes, and off they marched toward their rendezvous with history.

ARMY SECRETARY Wilber Brucker, shown at the Pentagon after Eisenhower's order which placed the Arkansas National Guard under Federal control, was instructed by the Defense secretary to use any other forces necessary to control the Little Rock situation.

MAJOR GENERAL Edwin A. Walker is commander of the federalized Arkansas National Guard and all regular army units ordered into Little Rock area. INP

Nearly all the fight and animosity appeared to have been blasted out of the remnants of the how I segregationists who two days ago

had threatened to harm the dents and forced Mayor row Wilson Mann, to send children home.

A few diehards yelled epit the departing backs of the N and their convoy.

An officer wheeled and an order: "Stay back!"

They stayed back.

The strange little process Negroes in search of an tion and troops grimly bent mission assigned by of the United States great caterpillar thro ing field of camerams porters.

ENTER FRONT

The students entered th campus and followed the pat the reflecting pool, and as the left stairway to the en to the school which Gov. Faubus and sometimes his supporters had arbitrarily verboten.

The steel-helmeed soldiers

(See Action on Page 2

Rae Foley's new

Action

(Continued from Page 8)

among 350 stationed outside the school.

There were another 24 inside the building to preserve order and Maj. Gen. Edwin A. Walker, 47-year-old commander of the troops, said they would be sent "elsewhere"

Historic *Chicago Defender* headline. (The newspaper made one mistake: September 25, 1957, was a Wednesday.)

There was some name-calling that day—Wednesday, September 25. But compared to their first experience in the school two days earlier, things went smoothly. One reason was that only 1,250 of Central's 2,000 students were in attendance. The rest had been kept home by their parents, some to protest school integration, others for fear of violence. Some white students had wanted to welcome the Nine but had been afraid of their racist classmates' reactions. The soldiers served as shields both for the Nine and for the white pupils who could now befriend them.

Shortly after noon an unidentified man phoned in a bomb threat. For thirty-three minutes, while soldiers and school employees searched to make sure there was no bomb, the students stood outside. During that time an *Arkansas Democrat* reporter called to Terrance Roberts, "How are you being treated?"

"Fine," he answered.

As they waited, Thelma Mothershed and Minnijean Brown talked with white students and a teacher. "Are you making any friends, Minnijean?" a reporter called from across the street.

"Quite a few," she said with a smile.

After school, when the Nine returned to her home, Daisy Bates asked about their day. Some of the white students had been friendly and had invited the black students to join them for lunch, they told her. Several of her classmates had invited her to sing in the glee club, Minnijean Brown cheerfully reported.

But Ernest Green seemed downcast, and Daisy Bates wanted to know why. "Sure we're in Central," Ernest said. "But how did we get in? We got in because we were protected by paratroopers. Some victory!"

One of the Nine asked Ernest if he was sorry that the president had sent in the troops. "No," he answered, "I'm just sorry it had to be that way."

Over the next few weeks it would become evident that Ernest's pessimism was justified.

September 25 *Arkansas Democrat* **bayonet photo.**

12

"See You Later, Integrator!"

During the few days that the 101st Airborne Division guarded the Nine, the situation remained under control at Central High. The soldiers made sure that no one outside the school interfered with integration, and within the building there were no major incidents.

"The Hundred and First were professional, disciplined soldiers," Elizabeth Eckford explained when we spoke to her.

"A soldier went from class to class with each of us and waited outside the door," added Thelma Mothershed Wair, who was a hundred-pound, four-foot eight-inch junior with heart problems when she helped integrate Central High in September 1957. "They [the racists] didn't do anything with the Hundred and First there."

But things soon changed.

On September 25 *The Arkansas Democrat* ran a front-page photo showing two soldiers moving two white teenage girls away from the Central High entrance. A close look at the photo reveals that the girls are laughing and that the soldiers' bayonets are not touching them. But because of the angle at which the photo was taken, a viewer not studying it closely could mistakenly think that one of the girls is being poked in the back by a bayonet point. This famous photo was put to use by the segregationists.

They printed small cards showing a white and a black child being herded together by soldiers' bayonets, accompanied by the words:

BROTHERHOOD BY BAYONET! START LOVING EACH
OTHER—THAT'S A COURT ORDER

Thousands of these cards were distributed in and beyond Little Rock. They stirred up so much rage in the South that several congressmen called Virgil Blossom to complain about the brutality of the U.S. soldiers at Central High.

Governor Faubus added fuel to the fire. On the night of Thursday, September 26, he appeared on national television and referred to his state as "an occupied territory." Designed to anger white southerners, this comment evoked images of the Reconstruction era after the Civil War, when the victorious North stationed troops in the southern states.

On October 1 the federalized Arkansas National Guard replaced the 101st Airborne troops at Central High. The U.S. government hoped that because the Guardsmen came from Arkansas, they would be less objectionable to white Little Rockians. The problem was, the Guardsmen tended to look the other way when the Nine were attacked.

"I never felt I was protected by the Arkansas National Guard," Elizabeth Eckford told us. "They were young, and hadn't been trained very well."

"Some of the National Guardsmen had gone to Central the year before and probably didn't want us at their school," added Thelma Mothershed Wair.

Compounding the problem was the fact that, each day, more of the students who had stayed out to protest integration returned to school. Among them were many of the hard-core troublemakers.

The result was that Tuesday, October 1, was a "terrible day" at school, Daisy Bates told the *Arkansas Gazette*. That morning a large crowd of students met the Nine at the front entrance. "Niggers, go home!" they shouted, throwing pencils and other objects. Things got worse that day, as the Nine were tripped, kicked, and sprayed with ink.

Melba Pattillo thought that the racists had assigned certain students to torment each of the Nine. One boy followed her through the halls, stepping on her heels until they bled. While Melba was in a bathroom stall, three girls held the door closed and threw flaming wads of paper at her. Choking from the smoke, Melba fought her way out of the stall.

The Arkansas National Guard knew what was happening but "looked on like spectators at a sports event—not like men sent to guard our safety," Melba reported. Because the bullies were "having a field day all over the place," as Daisy Bates put it, white students who had befriended the Nine were now afraid to do so. Before the day ended, the 101st was brought back to provide more protection at the school. But the Arkansas National Guard would do most of the monitoring of Central High for the rest of the school year.

Daisy Bates made sure that the nine students rode safely in Army vehicles and later in car pools to and from Central. But she was frustrated at being unable to

Jefferson Thomas (*left*) and Ernest Green study a September 1957 article about their attempt to attend Central High School.

protect them at school. Authorities ignored her demands that they do more to punish offenders, saying they could act only if an adult witnessed an incident, because otherwise it was just one student's word against another's. Naturally the racists did most of their bullying without eyewitnesses. The result was that during the entire school year only four white students were expelled from Central—despite hundreds of incidents of brutality.

Mrs. Bates tried to help the Nine in another way. The constant TV and newspaper coverage won them support among millions of people but made things worse for them at school. Their white classmates resented being portrayed as villains while the black students were generally hailed as heroes. Realizing this, Mrs. Bates mentioned in an October 3 conversation with NAACP officials in New York that she was trying to "cut down on the publicity," because "every time they print something about the kids, the kids have to face it the next day in school." It was useless, though, for the events at Central High were big news, as she could see by reading her mail.

Every week Daisy Bates received dozens of letters from near and far. She saved many of them. Nearly half a century later it is still unnerving to read some of the hate letters. For example, a postcard mailed from Rochester, Minnesota, on September 23, 1957, was addressed:

GRAND N.A.A.C.P.A. LEADER
N.I.G.G.A.R. ASSN
Little Rock, ARK.

Somehow the Little Rock post office delivered the card to Mrs. Bates. It bore the message:

Nuts to you Blacks
You haven't done a thing
here to warrent respect
Go back to Africa
Tom Cat

Like "Tom Cat," the most vicious racists generally didn't sign their real names. Some of the unsigned letters contained threats, such as the following:

Greer, S. Carolina
9/26/57

Dear "Nigger lover & Stupid"

    I thought you might want to know that I *hate, hate* you and what you stand for. Arkansas was one of the best states but when your stupid "Nigger" friends had to butt in and it is my belief that this is the beginning of the downfall of the United States of America. If our wonderful state, South Carolina has this problem I hope none of your "nigger friends" leaves this world but if it is necessary that might just happen. HA! HA!

A Nigger & N.A.A.C.P. Hater

Postcard received by Daisy Bates in September 1957.

A letter sent from Dallas, Texas, on September 24 proclaimed:

> I hope you read these few lines. For they are the Voice of Millions of
> People. You are a Hindrance to the Colored people. Surely you know
> by now, the white people Do Not Want Them, and Will Not Have
> them. Now or Never. May God Bless Governor Faubus.

A woman writing from an unknown location began by saying:

> I have been reading about the trouble your race are giving the people
> of Little Rock. When the U.S. brought your ancestors here from Africa
> they were not much more than savages the South has civilized.

Buried among her racist comments was an interesting observation: If Daisy
Bates thought blacks were treated so well in the North, she should visit some cities
such as Chicago or Detroit.

Some people claimed to have "scientific evidence" that integration was wrong.
Forgetting that we are all human beings regardless of our race, a letter writer in
Barcelona, Spain, advised Mrs. Bates that

> Segregation is the law of nature. With all the animals, including birds
> and insects, each species sticks to its own kind.

From Conway, Arkansas, came a letter from a person who had some strange
ideas about blood:

> So you believe in integration? That means that your white and black
> corpuscles have come together in the blood. Perhaps the white will
> absorb the black. Is that what you want to happen?

The many encouraging letters she received inspired Daisy Bates. Two of those she kept came from a man in New York City and a woman in Chicago, respectively:

Dear Mrs. Bates,

I am a white Southerner now living in New York. After reading in today's New York Times of your courageous work, I am moved to let you know that I am proud of you for your magnificent behavior in this dark hour of our country's history. Without you and others like you this would be an even darker hour indeed. You have the admiration of many outside of Little Rock who know that you are fighting the fight for all of us who believe in a more truly democratic America.

My dear Mrs. Bates,

In years to come when this is all part of the past, your brave children who are suffering so now, will go down as real heroes in the history of our country. Let me say on behalf of a great many other white people that we know there is no apology great enough to cover the cruelty you and your children have suffered, but we will do all we can to smooth the way for you.

Some white people declared that bigots disliked blacks only because they didn't know them. A Brooklyn, New York, woman wrote:

I am a teacher in a New York City school which is about fifty percent Negro and fifty percent white. Integration is both workable and desirable.

A white woman living outside St. Louis, Missouri, described how her family's black landlord and landlady had helped provide them with groceries and a job during hard times. The white students in Little Rock were bigoted only because of what they had been taught at home, this woman added. "Mrs. Bates, that's not the kids talking," she wrote. "That's their folks."

Letters came from other countries as well. From Enfield, England:

> May we, as a white English family, express to you our distress at the recent happenings in Little Rock, and wish you every success in your cause.

From Amsterdam, the Netherlands:

> This is to notify you how the Dutch nation admires your attitude and courage. Every modern human being here in Europe, being brown, black, white, yellow or whatever race, stands behind your opinions.

From Brantford, Ontario, Canada:

> Up here, we don't judge a person by the color of his skin. We believe superiority goes much deeper. It means civilized conduct, decency, charity, and above all tolerance. We have colored Canadians who are vastly superior than your bird brained Arkansas state governor.

These letter writers made two thought-provoking points about the Central High situation. First, it was true that there would be less conflict if the white and black students could get to know each other. This was proved in mid-October 1957, when NBC News broadcast a panel discussion among three black students (Melba Pattillo, Minnijean Brown, and Ernest Green) and four white students, including a girl who was a leader of the segregationists.

"What have you been taught that makes you just hate us so much?" Minnijean asked the white students.

They didn't hate the blacks, the white students answered. They just wanted them to go to their own school, and they resented the troops that had been sent into Central. Ernest then responded:

You say: Why did the troops come here? It is because our state government went against the federal law. Our country is set up so that we have forty-eight states and no one state has the ability to overrule our nation's government. I thought that was what our country was built around. I mean, that is why we fight. We fought in World War II together. The fellows that I know died in World War II, they died in the Korean War. I mean, why should my friends get out there and die for a cause called "democracy" when I can't exercise my rights? Tell me that.

By the end of the discussion the seven students had found some common ground. Even the girl who had been a segregationist ringleader conceded:

I know now that it isn't as bad as I thought it was—after we got together and discussed it. I think that's what they ought to do in

The Little Rock Nine gathered at the Bates home for a Thanksgiving celebration in 1957. From left: Terrance Roberts, Melba Pattillo, Thelma Mothershed, L.C. Bates, and Daisy Bates.

Central. They ought to have a panel discussion or something like that to let all of the kids know—not just a few but all of the kids.

The other thought-provoking comment was that the white youngsters were being influenced by "their folks," as the woman from outside St. Louis told Daisy Bates. Parents who belonged to the Mothers' League and the Capital Citizens' Council convinced their sons and daughters that it was heroic to fight integration. Governor Faubus reinforced this view by portraying white Arkansans as underdogs standing up to the mighty federal government. As a result some white students saw themselves as "brave young soldiers" fighting for their parents, their governor, their state, and their way of life by opposing integration in their high school.

A white youth named Joe talked about this during the NBC panel discussion. "If parents would just stay out of it and let the children at Central High figure it out for themselves, I think it would be a whole lot better," Joe argued. "I think the students are mature enough to figure it out for themselves."

At school, however, things were getting worse instead of better. On Wednesday, October 2, a group of about fifty white students chased Jefferson Thomas and Terrance Roberts through the corridors. When they caught up to Jefferson and Terrance, some boys knocked their books out of their hands. As the two students bent down to retrieve their books, they were punched and kicked. A white girl who witnessed this attack told the *Arkansas Gazette* that an Arkansas National Guardsman looked on but did nothing. Fortunately, Assistant Principal Elizabeth Huckaby also saw what happened, and three white boys were suspended for their actions. One of them bragged to the *Gazette:* "We wanted to make it so miserable, they would not want to go to the school."

Violence against the Nine ranged from thumbtacks placed on their chairs to serious attacks. "We were assaulted every day in school, and no one came to our aid," recalls Elizabeth Eckford. "We were body slammed into lockers and our lockers were vandalized. They tripped us on the stairs, walked on our heels, and hit the boys with wet towels." Thelma Mothershed Wair has memories of being stuck with safety pins. "They'd call me 'nigger' and say, 'Why don't you go back to Africa?'"

All of the Nine endured psychological and verbal abuse. The pro-segregation students organized "stare days," when dozens of them would silently stare at the Nine all day, and "black days," when they would come to school dressed completely in black to protest the presence of the Nine. The youthful bigots walked around yelling, "See you later, integrator!" and the ever-present "Two, four, six, eight, we ain't gonna integrate!" Messages such as "NIGGER GO HOME" were written in lipstick on bathroom walls. Cards containing racist messages and rhymes, many of them printed by adults, appeared everywhere:

PERMIT
GOOD INDEFINITELY
BEARER MAY FREELY AND ENERGETICALLY KICK THE RUMPS
OF VIRGIL BLOSSOM [AND] DAISY BATES

PERMIT
GOOD UNTIL MAY 29, 1958
BEARER MAY KICK RUMPS
OF EACH CHS NEGRO ONCE PER DAY
SIGNED: DAISY BLOSSOM

LITTLE NIGGER AT CENTRAL HIGH
HAS GOT MIGHTY FREE WITH HIS EYE,
WINKS AT WHITE GIRLS,
GRABS THEIR BLOND CURLS:
LITTLE NIGGER IS ANXIOUS TO DIE

By making anonymous telephone threats, the racists tried to scare the school board into closing Central High. During the 1957–58 school year Central received at least forty-three credible bomb threats. Each time, a ten-man crew had to search the building from top to bottom. On three occasions homemade bombs actually were found in the building. Two sticks of dynamite were also discovered during school hours, and students set at least thirty fires in wastebaskets and lockers.

Hundreds of anonymous phone calls were also made to the families of the Nine and to Daisy Bates. "People would call us, threatening to burn our house down," Thelma Mothershed Wair recalls. "We had to take the phone off the hook, otherwise we couldn't sleep." One day Terrance Roberts's mother, who ran a catering service, received a call that her son had been seriously hurt at school. When she

In this Bill Mauldin cartoon, a soldier compares his Little Rock ribbon to one earned in a foreign conflict.

"No, *this* is my Lebanon ribbon. The other one is for Little Rock."

August 6, 1958

110

arrived at the principal's office, Mrs. Roberts was relieved to find that the call had been a hoax.

The patrol at Central High was reduced to only a few Arkansas National Guardsmen on November 11. That set the stage for one of the year's most brutal incidents. On Tuesday, November 12, Jefferson Thomas was standing by his locker when a couple of white boys, pushing and shoving each other, approached. Jefferson kept an eye on the boys, because one of the racists' tricks was to "play fight" near a black student and then "accidentally" crash into him or her with elbows and legs flying. If caught, the whites would insist that they had just been "horsing around" and hadn't intended to hurt anybody. As Jefferson watched the boys, another boy came up behind him and hit him so hard on his head that he crumpled to the floor, unconscious.

A teacher heard the commotion and ran out of a classroom to revive Jefferson and help him to Principal Jess Matthews's office. Daisy Bates was called and informed of the attack, but because her presence at school might spark a riot, she asked NAACP official Clarence Laws to go get Jefferson. Mr. Laws took Jefferson to a doctor for treatment. Then he drove him to the home of Mrs. Bates, who flew into a rage when she saw the huge lump on the side of Jefferson's head.

The next morning she phoned Jefferson's home to ask how he was, only to learn that he was going to school. If the thugs knew that they could bully him into staying home, Jefferson felt, it would just encourage them. By this time everyone knew the identity of Jefferson's attacker because the boy had been boasting about it. Checking the notes she had made during her daily after-school sessions with the Nine, Daisy Bates saw that the boy who had struck Jefferson had been involved in many previous incidents.

It was time to confront the superintendent, Daisy Bates decided. By nine A.M. she and Clarence Laws were at Virgil Blossom's office. Mrs. Bates showed him the records she had kept of attacks on the Nine and asked what he intended to do about the violence. "If you are really interested in clearing up this trouble," she told Mr. Blossom, "you should expel some of these troublemakers."

But Mr. Blossom thought she was exaggerating the problem and apparently

During the 1957–58 school crisis, Daisy Bates gave speeches about events in Little Rock; this advertisement was for a presentation in Baltimore, Maryland.

told her to take up the matter with the National Guard. "You can't tell me how to run my schools!" he added.

"It's up to you to maintain discipline inside the school," Mrs. Bates retorted. "By not doing so you are subjecting the children to physical torture that you will have to live with the rest of your life." She and Mr. Laws stormed out of the superintendent's office.

That afternoon when the Nine came over to discuss the day's events, Mrs. Bates learned that conditions were going from bad to worse. Melba and Carlotta had been kicked, Ernest had been hit in the face with hot towels in the shower room after gym, Jefferson had been knocked down in gym and nearly pushed into the steam pipes, and Elizabeth had signed out of school early because some girls had smashed her with basketballs in gym and the teacher had ignored it.

Daisy Bates spoke to generals and U.S. officials, but no one wanted to take responsibility. It was the school's job to discipline troublemakers, the Arkansas National Guard claimed. The National Guard was there to protect the black students, insisted school officials. After his initial toughness, President Eisenhower pulled back from the Central High crisis.

"Most people turned their backs," Elizabeth Eckford recalls of those difficult days nearly half a century ago. "The authorities didn't hear what they heard, and didn't see what they saw."

Daisy Bates continued to speak out, and was quoted by the Associated Press news service as saying that the Nine were "being bullied and harassed to try to force them to leave. But they're not going to give in."

Her outspokenness helped. Two guards from the 101st Airborne were temporarily assigned to each of the Nine during the school day, which improved the situation—at least for a while.

"MRS" DAISY BATES
Little Rock's "Lady" of The Year
(SEE POLICE RECORD BELOW)

CENTRAL HIGH SCHOOL'S MOST PROMINENT P.T.A. MEMBER, SELF-APPOINTED PROTECTOR OF NINE NEGRO CHILDREN, HAVING RECEIVED "SUBPOENA" POWERS FROM JESS MATTHEWS, CENTRAL HIGH SCHOOL PRINCIPAL, AND ALSO AUTHORITY TO CROSS EXAMINE WHITE STUDENTS, UNOFFICIAL "PRINCIPAL" IN CHARGE OF LECTURING WHITE STUDENTS AT CENTRAL HIGH WHO "CROSS" ANY OF HER "BRAVE" NINE NEGRO STUDENTS.

DAISY BATES - SHERIFF'S OFFICE PHOTOS

Flyer distributed by the Capital Citizens' Council.

13

"Follow in Your Footsteps"

While the Nine were being tormented at school, Daisy Bates was also under attack. On Halloween of 1957 the Little Rock City Council ordered that she be arrested for refusing to answer Attorney General Bruce Bennett's questions about the NAACP members.

Mrs. Bates turned herself in the next day—November 1—and was released on bail. At her trial in early December in Little Rock's Municipal Court, Judge Harry Robinson ruled against her. Saying "She heads some branch or something in the NAACP," Judge Robinson ordered her to pay a $100 fine. Instead of paying, she and her NAACP lawyers took the case to two higher courts in Arkansas, where they also lost. Not until 1960 would the United States Supreme Court rule that Arkansas officials had violated Daisy Bates's freedom of speech by demanding that she provide private information about the NAACP.

Back in 1946 Daisy and L.C. Bates had been arrested for contempt of court for criticizing a judge in their newspaper. Mrs. Bates also had been arrested several other times on what appear to have been trumped-up charges. For example, in 1952 she had been arrested for betting on a card game. The Capital Citizens' Council obtained Daisy Bates's arrest record as well as a photograph from her 1946 contempt arrest, and made up a flyer showing her mug shot and rap sheet. The flyer, which was distributed around Little Rock, made it appear that

Daisy Bates was a criminal. What was especially disturbing was that the police had evidently helped the Capital Citizens' Council prepare the flyer.

The Bates home also continued to be the target of violence—despite the volunteers who guarded it at night. Crosses were repeatedly burned on the Bates property. The burning of a cross has long been a trademark of the Ku Klux Klan, a white hate group whose members hide their identities behind robes and hoods. Formed in the 1860s, the KKK was known for terrorizing, torturing, and murdering black people, so the cross burnings had to be taken seriously. Several attempts were made to set the Bates house on fire, one when a kind of firebomb called a Molotov cocktail was thrown into the carport. In addition, a carload of hoodlums fired a gun at the home. One bullet burst through the already broken window and stuck in a living room wall, but it didn't hit anyone.

"We experienced the horrifying feeling that in our own home town there lived people who wanted us dead," Daisy Bates wrote.

David E. Neely, the son of L.C.'s cousin Lottie Brown Neely, recalls the dangers the Bateses faced in the late 1950s. Born in Chicago in 1952, David periodically

Arkansas State Press article about cross burnings on the Bateses' property.

drove down to Arkansas with his family to visit cousins L.C. and Daisy. In his Chicago law office Mr. Neely described what it was like to be in the Bates home nearly fifty years ago, when he was five or six years old:

"I was there when bricks came through the window. I heard screaming. I saw fire." David Neely also remembers seeing flyers predicting that Daisy Bates would soon be "pushing up daisies"—meaning she would be dead. "My earliest impressions of Little Rock were that it was violent and full of people who hated Daisy Bates."

He also has vivid memories of his cousin Daisy. "She was brave. She was always focused and would never turn away from the main issue. My impression was of a beautiful woman who was always on the go, always getting phone calls, always with people around her."

Some of those people were prominent civil rights leaders. Daisy Bates became close friends with Rosa Parks, who had refused to relinquish her bus seat to a white passenger in Montgomery, Alabama, in 1955. Dr. Martin Luther King Jr., who organized the Montgomery bus boycott after Mrs. Parks's brave action, was at the Bates home. David Neely remembers sitting on Dr. King's lap, and he dimly recalls a discussion between Dr. King and NAACP head Roy Wilkins, with whom L.C. had worked on the *Kansas City Call*. Mr. Neely also remembers visits by NAACP lawyer Thurgood Marshall, who would become the U.S. Supreme Court's first black justice; Whitney Young, who would establish the school program Head Start; and labor leader A. Philip Randolph, who would organize the 1963 March on Washington at which Dr. King would make his "I Have a Dream" speech.

The civil rights leaders visited the Bateses to help plan strategy and to show support for them and the nine black students. They slipped in and out of Little Rock quietly, so that the racists wouldn't complain about "outside agitators" coming to stir up trouble. Often they stayed in the Bates home, along with out-of-town reporters. L.C. and Daisy set up beds in their downstairs den, where Dr. King, Thurgood Marshall, and others sometimes spent the night.

Daisy Bates arranged for her famous friends and acquaintances to give the Nine pep talks. On the evening of October 17, 1957, six of the Nine, two of their

Dr. Martin Luther King Jr.

mothers, reporter Ted Poston, and Daisy Bates had a long telephone conversation with Jackie Robinson, who had retired as a major league baseball player the previous year. The following is a portion of the conversation, which Robinson participated in from NAACP headquarters in New York:

> DAISY BATES: This is Minnijean Brown. She is sixteen years old.
> MINNIJEAN BROWN: I would like to say that what we are doing is following the example you gave us, and we are trying to follow in your footsteps.
> JACKIE ROBINSON: I don't feel there is anyone who could have done

118

the job you youngsters are doing. We wish we could participate in some way, but we would just throw more pressure on you than you already have.

DAISY BATES: This is Thelma Mothershed. Thelma, would you like to say hello to Mr. Robinson?

THELMA MOTHERSHED: Hello, Mr. Robinson.

JACKIE ROBINSON: Hello, Thelma. We are getting along wonderfully well up here. We are all puffed up because of the job the youngsters are doing in Little Rock.

DAISY BATES: This is Melba Pattillo, the actress of the group.

JACKIE ROBINSON: I know everybody up here and in Little Rock is saying that you youngsters have shown the world how people can conduct themselves under pressure, and certainly you at your age shouldn't have to face this.

MELBA PATTILLO: Well, thank you, thank you, sir, it has been a pleasure talking with you.

DAISY BATES: Here is Carlotta Walls.

CARLOTTA WALLS: Hello, Mr. Robinson.

JACKIE ROBINSON: I think it is one of the finest things that could happen, talking to you. I think it makes my job look like nothing, what I had to go through. I had a little bit more age on you. Many people all over the world are talking about you. . . . People will be talking about this for years to come.

Perhaps their civil rights friends suggested a strategy that L.C. and Daisy used in their newspaper. To convince Little Rockians that integration was an everyday, easily achieved process, they tried to paint a rosy picture of conditions at Central High. For example, the November 15, 1957, *State Press* declared: "CALMNESS REPLACES TERROR AT CHS AS U.S. TROOPS GRADUALLY WITHDRAW." This was three days after Jefferson Thomas had been knocked unconscious. To northern reporters who sympathized with the Nine, however, Daisy Bates revealed how bad things were at the school.

THE POWER OF ONE

Telephone
MUrray Hill 2-0500

Chock full o' Nuts

425 LEXINGTON AVENUE
New York 17, N. Y.

THE WHITE HOUSE
MAY 14 11 36 AM '58
RECEIVED

May 13, 1958

The President
The White House
Washington, D. C.

My dear Mr. President:

I was sitting in the audience at the Summit Meeting of Negro
Leaders yesterday when you said we must have patience. On
hearing you say this, I felt like standing up and saying, "Oh
no! Not again."

I respectfully remind you sir, that we have been the most
patient of all people. When you said we must have self-
respect, I wondered how we could have self-respect and remain patient considering the treatment accorded us through
the years.

17 million Negroes cannot do as you suggest and wait for the
hearts of men to change. We want to enjoy now the rights
that we feel we are entitled to as Americans. This we cannot do unless we pursue aggressively goals which all other
Americans achieved over 150 years ago.

As the chief executive of our nation, I respectfully suggest
that you unwittingly crush the spirit of freedom in Negroes
by constantly urging forbearance and give hope to those pro-
segregation leaders like Governor Faubus who would take
from us even those freedoms we now enjoy. Your own experience with Governor Faubus is proof enough that forbearance and not eventual integration is the goal the pro-
segregation leaders seek.

In my view, an unequivocal statement backed up by action
such as you demonstrated you could take last fall in deal-

Letter from Jackie Robinson to President Eisenhower asserting that African Americans "want to enjoy now the rights that we feel we are entitled to as Americans."

Mrs. Bates constantly reminded the Nine to ignore the taunts and go about their business. Except for each other and a small number of white students, the Nine had few people to talk to at Central High and sometimes felt almost invisible. "It was a lonely existence," Thelma Mothershed Wair remembers. Melba Pattillo Beals described how she felt in *Warriors Don't Cry*:

> I longed for someone to acknowledge that I was alive by saying something pleasant to me, and allowing me to say something back. Sometimes when a classmate said something funny, I would smile and even laugh out loud. "We weren't talking to you, nigger," they would say. Jolted back to reality by their cruelty, I would catch myself, hide my feelings, and stare straight ahead. "Nigger," I would whisper to remind myself. That's all I am to them. They don't see me as a real person. There even came a moment when I pinched myself to see if I was really there. So many times I wanted to shout, "I'm Melba, don't you see me? I play the piano, I can make blouses, I can write poems, and I sing."

One of the Nine, Minnijean Brown, didn't always ignore the taunts. A friendly and outspoken young lady, Minnijean was so wounded by the insults that she sometimes yelled back at her tormentors. Seeing that they could get a rise out of Minnijean, the bigots decided to target her for special abuse.

In the late fall of 1957 Minnijean received more than the usual amount of kicks, threats, and insults. Convinced that her classmates would like her if they heard how beautifully she sang, Minnijean decided to try out for the Christmas talent show. "She delighted in planning for the performance," Melba Pattillo explained, "displaying a joyful glee about the possibility of singing in front of the white kids."

The prospect of a black student appearing in the talent show sparked a protest from Margaret Jackson, president of the Mothers' League of Central High School. Mrs. Jackson needn't have worried, for school officials weren't allowing any of the Nine to take part in extracurricular activities. Minnijean was disappointed and frustrated that she couldn't even try out for the Christmas program.

Imogene Brown was so upset about her daughter's exclusion that she went with Daisy Bates to meet with Principal Jess Matthews. The conference was held on Monday, December 9. Mrs. Bates gave Mr. Matthews an earful. She chided him for not allowing Minnijean to perform in the Christmas show, accused him of ignoring Minnijean's especially cruel treatment, and criticized him for not preparing the white students to accept integration. School officials were doing their best under difficult conditions, Mr. Matthews replied.

The Christmas season brought a new kind of torment for the Nine. Some students went around school singing a distorted version of "White Christmas," substituting the word "Central" for "Christmas." Principal Matthews even had to step in and ban a student group from performing the song at the Christmas program. This prompted Mothers' League president Margaret Jackson to place an advertisement in the *Arkansas Democrat* complaining:

GOODBYE "WHITE CHRISTMAS" AT CENTRAL HIGH SCHOOL:
Mr. Matthews, how far shall the white people be expected to go
in appeasing the whims of the African race?

Mrs. Jackson neglected to mention that the students intended to change the words to "I'm dreaming of a white Central."

Christmas vacation was to begin after school on Wednesday, December 18. The day before, Minnijean Brown entered the cafeteria with Melba, Ernest, and two other black students. At lunchtime the Nine were more vulnerable than usual, for the cafeteria was huge and difficult for the staff to monitor.

Tuesday was chili day at Central. The others were already seated at a table while Minnijean went through the line to buy her lunch. As she headed toward the table with her tray, a group of boys blocked her path, sticking out their feet and shoving chairs in her way to try to trip her, all the while calling her names.

Suddenly, Minnijean's frustration boiled over. She flipped her tray and dumped the chili on the heads of two white boys.

The cafeteria went quiet as everyone turned to see what had happened. The two boys with chili dripping down their faces and the hundreds of onlookers seemed astonished that Minnijean had struck back. Watching with the other black students from a table, Melba "wondered whether we'd ever get out of there alive" because of the wrath of the whites. The sound of a few hands clapping broke the silence. The lunchroom workers, who were black, had seen what had occurred and were applauding Minnijean.

Within moments a school official appeared. Minnijean and the four other black students were rushed out of the cafeteria to prevent any more trouble. Minnijean was taken to the principal's office. It turned out that in her anger Minnijean had apparently dumped the chili on two boys who hadn't been among those heckling her or blocking her path. The two boys weren't angry, insisting that Minnijean had been picked on so often they "didn't blame her for getting mad." Nevertheless, Principal Matthews suspended Minnijean for six school days for the chili dumping. Since Christmas vacation was about to begin, she wouldn't be allowed back to Central until Monday, January 13, 1958. As part of the conditions for her readmission, she agreed that in the future she would speak to school authorities rather than retaliate against physical or verbal threats.

Hoping to provoke another outburst that would get Minnijean expelled from school permanently, the bigots resumed their harassment upon her return. On Thursday, January 16, 1958, a boy dumped a bowl of soup on Minnijean. "Oh, well, they got even with me," she told Elizabeth Eckford, with whom she was eating. Minnijean told Assistant Principal Mrs. Elizabeth Huckaby what had happened, and the soup dumper was suspended for three days.

"MRS. BATES SAYS 9 NEGROES WON'T QUIT DESPITE TROUBLE," an *Arkansas Gazette* headline proclaimed on January 29. After school that day a boy came up behind Minnijean and kicked her viciously as she walked to her mother's car. Two teachers and an Arkansas National Guardsman witnessed this attack, which hurt

Carlotta Walls (*left*) and Minnijean Brown arrive at school.

Minnijean so badly, she had to miss two days of school. Daisy Bates wanted the boy arrested, but law enforcement officials said it was a school matter. Yet because the boy was already serving a suspension for cutting classes and the attack occurred outside the building after regular hours, school authorities claimed it was not their responsibility and did little about it.

As Daisy Bates feared, Minnijean Brown had again reached the breaking point. On the afternoon of Thursday, February 6, Minnijean walked into the Bates house with some bad news. Pacing back and forth as she spoke, she told Mrs. Bates that a girl had been calling her names for days. "When I entered the building this morning," she said, "this girl followed me, kicking me on the legs and calling me names. As we were entering our homeroom, she called out, 'black bitch.' I turned and screamed, 'White trash! If you weren't white trash, you wouldn't bother me!'" The

124

white girl threw her pocketbook at Minnijean, hitting her in the head. Minnijean picked up the pocketbook and was about to hurl it back at the girl but then thought better of it. "I threw the bag on the floor in front of her and walked away."

"I'm glad you were able to restrain yourself," Daisy Bates said.

But it didn't do Minnijean any good. She and the white girl were taken to Principal Matthews, who offered to overlook the matter if they promised to avoid each other in the future. Minnijean agreed, but the white girl refused and transferred to another school. Minnijean was then expelled from Central High. The official explanation was that she had called the girl "white trash" after agreeing not to retaliate against harassment, but the real reason was that school authorities feared Minnijean's presence would provoke more violence.

Everyone knew that Minnijean's expulsion was unfair. Elizabeth Huckaby wrote: "The truth, of course, was that we could no longer run the school if Minnijean was there. She and our impossible situation would not mix."

Following her expulsion, Minnijean was quoted in newspapers as saying that she had been left with only one white girl friend at the end, because the racists had pressured other white students into avoiding her. "Make that half a friend," she corrected. "When she's with me, she's my friend. When she's with the white students, she acts differently." Summarizing the abuse she had endured, Minnijean added: "They throw rocks, they spill ink on your clothes, they call you 'nigger,' they just keep bothering you every five minutes."

Daisy Bates thought Minnijean should continue her education far from Little Rock. She helped arrange for her to move to New York City, where Minnijean would attend the New Lincoln High School while living with the family of famed black psychologist Dr. Kenneth Clark. The racists hounded Minnijean to the last moment. On the February day that she departed for New York, her flight had to be delayed due to a bomb threat.

The bigots celebrated Minnijean's expulsion. Cards boasting ONE DOWN . . . EIGHT TO GO were printed and passed out at Central High. But Daisy Bates was determined that all eight remaining students would complete the last three months of school.

A mother and son parade in front of the Arkansas State Capitol.

14

"We Made It"

The segregationists followed through on their threat to destroy the *State Press* if the Bateses kept fighting for integration. They pressured firms to stop advertising in the newspaper. Companies that refused were intimidated. For example, a grocer received an anonymous phone threat that his store would be bombed if he ran any more ads in the Bateses' paper. That same night three rough-looking men entered his store and stood staring at the shelves in a menacing way. The frightened grocer cancelled his advertising contract with the *State Press*.

Even worse, the newspaper's circulation plunged. At one time about 40 percent of the newspaper's subscribers had been white. Hundreds of white readers cancelled their *State Press* subscriptions because they opposed its pro-integration stance. Others cancelled because they feared reprisals from bigots if they were seen getting the paper. Many blacks cancelled their subscriptions because their employers threatened to fire them if they didn't. In parts of Arkansas, African Americans were beaten up just for selling or reading the *State Press*. By early 1958 the paper was on the verge of collapse.

Daisy and her husband had yet another problem. Because their home had been the target of so many attempted fires and bombings, their household insurance was cancelled. This meant that if their home were destroyed, they would suffer a total loss.

At school the new year brought little change. The black students continued to be called names, tripped, and shoved in the hallways. Their lockers were vandalized repeatedly, and their books and other belongings were stolen.

Boys on motorcycles threw an iron pipe at the car in which Carlotta Walls and Gloria Ray were riding to school. Jefferson Thomas and Terrance Roberts were spat on while walking through a hallway. Daisy Bates recorded in her notes that on February 4, 1958, Terrance was close to withdrawing from Central. "I've had it!" he said when the students gathered at the Bates home that afternoon. "Today, during study hall, two boys kicked me. One was the same boy who kicked Jeff last week. When I reported them to the office, I was asked if a teacher saw them kick me. Unless we have an adult witness, nothing will be done no matter what they do to us."

"If you decide not to go back, I will understand," said Mrs. Bates, although she hoped that Terrance would change his mind.

Terrance returned to school the next morning. "I decided I wasn't going to let that pip-squeak chase me out of Central," he explained to Daisy Bates.

On February 14, 1958, snow covered the ground in Little Rock. As Thelma Mothershed and some friends entered school on that Valentine's Day, they were bombarded by rock-filled snowballs. Thelma was hit so hard that she burst into tears. The attack was repeated after school. When Oscar Eckford, Elizabeth's father, rushed from his car to try to stop the snowball throwers, he was pelted too.

Melba Pattillo was warned that, because she had been close friends with Minnijean, the bigots planned to get rid of her next. They repeatedly tried to provoke her. Raw eggs were dumped on Melba's head. A girl slapped and spat on her. She was tripped down a flight of stairs. Melba took her grandmother's advice and dealt with the bigots in an unusual way. Whenever they mistreated her, she said, "Thank you," and smiled sweetly at them. Not able to get a rise out of Melba, the bigots eased up their campaign against her.

In early April—just before spring break—Gloria Ray was informed that the next day some boys would squirt acid at her with water pistols. She and the others had received so many threats all year that she did not tell her parents about

Daisy Bates in her backyard.

this latest warning. Unknown to Gloria, a midnight caller claiming to be a friendly white parent phoned her mother with similar information about the acid threat. "If I were you I'd keep my daughter at home," the woman advised. At first Mary Ray figured this was just another caller trying to scare her into withdrawing Gloria from Central, but the more she thought about it, the more worried she became. In the morning Mrs. Ray phoned Daisy Bates to voice her concerns. Mrs. Bates called the school, but by the time she was put through to an administrator, it was too late.

Early in the school day Gloria was walking away from her locker when a group of boys who were notorious troublemakers blocked her path. She hurried off around a corner, where a boy with a water pistol suddenly appeared. Gloria closed her eyes just before he squirted her in the face. Only after frantically wiping away the liquid with the hem of her dress did Gloria realize it was just water. As she told

Mrs. Bates the story and relived the moment when she thought she had been disfigured by acid, tears streamed from Gloria's eyes.

With the end of the school year approaching, there was talk around Central High that the racists were saving their most violent act for last. The lone senior among the group, Ernest Green, was about to graduate. They wouldn't permit that to happen, the racists boasted.

Two graduation ceremonies were scheduled. At the baccalaureate service on Sunday, May 25, Central High's 602 graduating seniors were to hear a sermon by a minister. Two days later they were to receive their diplomas. Both ceremonies were to take place at the school's football stadium.

Rumors circulated that bombs would be hidden at the stadium. There was also talk that snipers with high-powered rifles would shoot Ernest from the windows of homes overlooking the field.

Around May 1, Ernest confided to Daisy Bates that he was scared. "Mrs. Bates," he asked, "do you know whether the police or the National Guard will be at our graduation? Today everyone was saying I won't be allowed to march with the graduating class. They say it like boasting."

Ernest Green's graduation would be a landmark in the civil rights struggle, Daisy Bates knew. If he were prevented from graduating, school integration might grind to a halt for years in Little Rock and other cities. But if he became the first black student at Little Rock's Central High School to receive his diploma, it would pave the way for thousands of black students to follow in his footsteps.

The week after Ernest confessed his fears to her, Mrs. Bates went to Washington, D.C. While in the nation's capital, she spoke to Army officials and others about protecting Ernest at the graduation ceremonies.

There was a burst of trouble in the days before graduation. On Thursday, May 8, a serious rock fight occurred outside the school between Central students and black pupils from Dunbar Junior High who were walking to a track meet. On Tuesday, May 13, several youths who didn't attend Central exploded a series of firecrackers in the school. The next day, May 14, Terrance Roberts was hit in the head by a rock as he walked from the field house to the main school building. The blow raised a huge bump on his head, yet Terrance refused to go home. By late May the school was so out of control that the black students were regularly pelted with rocks and rotten eggs as they entered or exited the building.

Finally, the end of school was at hand. Just before the graduation ceremonies, Melba Pattillo recorded her prayer in her diary:

> Dear God,
>   Please walk with Ernie in the graduation line at Central. Let him be safe.

Thanks partly to Mrs. Bates's efforts, authorities went to great lengths to protect Ernest. The FBI investigated the upper windows of houses near the stadium for potential sniper positions. Large numbers of National Guardsmen were stationed beneath the stands, and Little Rock policemen were in the crowd.

At the baccalaureate service on Sunday, May 25, there was only one incident. As the ceremony ended, a white member of the graduating class spat in the face of a young black girl who had come as Ernest's guest. Little Rock Assistant Police Chief Gene Smith witnessed the incident and arrested the boy.

Two days later the *Arkansas Gazette* pleaded with Little Rock citizens: "Let This Night Be Marked with Dignity." That night at the diploma ceremony many police, both uniformed and in plain clothes, were among the audience at the stadium. Dr. Martin Luther King Jr. considered Ernest's graduation so important that he came to Little Rock to see it, taking a seat with the other spectators in the stands.

The graduates were called alphabetically, each walking up a ramp to the platform to receive a diploma. The crowd of nearly 5,000 people became very quiet when it was time for Ernest Green's row to stand. Ernest's name was called, and the crowd watched him walk alone to the platform and accept his diploma. There were a few whistles and insulting comments from the stands, but nothing worse. Ernest Green returned to his seat with his diploma—the first black graduate of Central High School in Little Rock, Arkansas.

In late May 1958 Ernest Green became the first black graduate of Central High School.

Since each graduate had been allowed only eight tickets for family and friends, thousands of people listened to the ceremony on the radio. Among those who tuned in was Melba Pattillo, who later expressed what Ernest's graduation meant to black people:

> At 8:48 P.M., Ernie became the first of our people to graduate from Central High School. Chills danced up my spine as I sat in the big green living room chair with Mama and Grandma nearby. "It really happened," I whispered. "We made it."
>
> The audience had been applauding those who previously marched, but when Ernie appeared they fell silent.
>
> "What the heck," Mother said. "Lots of people in the rest of the world are applauding for Ernie and for all of you who made it through this year."
>
> "Who cares if they applaud, they didn't shoot him." Grandma stood and applauded.

After the graduation ceremony ended, Ernest was escorted by police to a waiting taxi, in which he and his relatives departed. Two days later, on May 29, the historic school year ended.

Black leaders greet Mrs. Bates as she arrives in Chicago.

15

"To Rid Our Nation of the Evils of Segregation"

Daisy Bates and the eight students did not end the school year feeling triumphant. They were more like long-distance runners, relieved to have finished a grueling race still on their feet. They had no time to rest, for civil rights groups in several cities wanted to honor them. As soon as school ended, Mrs. Bates and the young people flew off to Chicago. Minnijean Brown met them there, and for a while the Little Rock Nine were reunited. In the Windy City the group received the Robert S. Abbott Civil Rights Award, named for the publisher of the influential black newspaper the *Chicago Defender*.

In New York City the Nine were honored at Brooklyn's Concord Baptist Church and by a labor union. They dined with New York's governor, were welcomed to City Hall by the mayor, and were taken backstage at a Broadway play to meet famed performer Lena Horne. They also visited the Statue of Liberty, which Daisy Lee and her little white girl friend in Huttig had dreamed of doing forty years earlier.

Next came Washington, D.C. There they were given a private tour of the White House and posed on the steps of the United States Supreme Court with Thurgood Marshall.

The tour was a welcome break after the hardships of the school year. It was "a relief to get away from Little Rock," Elizabeth Eckford recalled. In her autobiography, Melba Pattillo Beals added:

New York City Mayor Robert Wagner meets the Little Rock Nine. Front row (*left to right*): Minnijean Brown, Elizabeth Eckford, Carlotta Walls, Mayor Wagner, Thelma Mothershed, Gloria Ray. Back row (*left to right*): Terrance Roberts, Ernest Green, Melba Pattillo, and Jefferson Thomas.

> In Little Rock we had been "niggers," but up North, we were heroes and heroines. We were paraded across stages before adoring audiences, chauffeured about in limousines, and treated like royalty at luxurious hotels.

The summer's big event came on July 11, 1958, during the NAACP's forty-ninth annual convention in Cleveland, Ohio. On that Friday night Daisy Bates and the Little Rock Nine were presented with the NAACP's prestigious Spingarn Medal, which had been instituted in 1914 for the "highest or noblest achievement by an American Negro." Two years earlier, in 1956, Jackie Robinson had received the award for his pioneering role in baseball, and in 1957 Dr. Martin Luther King Jr. had been given the medal for his leadership in the Montgomery bus boycott. The

1958 award, which Mrs. Bates and the Nine received for upholding the ideals of American democracy, marked the first time that the Spingarn Medal had been presented to a group.

> *I accept with humility this medal not for myself, for I was only privileged to be an instrument in a vast movement to rid our nation of the evils of segregation,*

Daisy Bates began in her acceptance speech.

> *I accept this medal as a tribute to all the people of the South—Negro and white—who want our country to be in truth the land of the free. I have been conscious of the moral support of millions of my fellow Americans, and it has given courage to the children, to their parents, and to me during the eight-month ordeal.*

She also had a warning. Educators, lawmakers, and law enforcers must do more to make sure the Supreme Court's integration order was carried out, so that "there will never be a repetition of Little Rock." She finished with words of hope:

> *Oft-times it seems that the wheels of justice turn slowly—but turn they must as long as we have young people such as these whom you are honoring here tonight, exemplifying courage, vision, and dedication not only for the cause of democracy in Arkansas, but that mankind around the world may enjoy dignity and freedom. If people of good will of both races get together in determination to maintain law and order, I am convinced that school desegregation will proceed as smoothly as it did in Louisville, Austin, Oklahoma City, and in scores of other communities throughout the South.*

Over the next year the "wheels of justice" turned more slowly in Little Rock than even Daisy Bates had expected. In the summer of 1958 Governor Orval Faubus pushed through six new state laws granting him broad powers to combat integration. One new law permitted the governor to close the schools rather than have them integrated by court order.

Meanwhile, the Little Rock School Board was trying to bring integration to a halt. The board went to court requesting a two-and-a-half-year "cooling-off period" during which there would be *no* school integration. On September 12, 1958, the U.S. Supreme Court ordered that there be no such cooling-off period. The Blossom Plan, which began integration at the high school level before working down to the lower grades, must go forward.

Invoking his new power, Governor Faubus ordered Little Rock's four high schools closed as of eight A.M. Monday, September 15, 1958. He was doing so, he said, because he believed that "violence is impending if Negroes are admitted to Central" for the new school year. He blamed the Arkansas NAACP president for the school turmoil. "If Daisy Bates would find an honest job, and if the U.S. Supreme Court would keep its cotton-picking hands off the Little Rock School Board's affairs, we could open the Little Rock schools!"

The high schools remained closed for the entire 1958–59 school year. Some students continued their educations by attending private schools or schools in other towns. Some took high school courses through the mail. But out of approximately 4,000 high school pupils in Little Rock, about 1,000 dropped out and never returned. Many were African Americans who couldn't afford to attend private schools or travel to schools far from home.

With Minnijean gone and Ernest having graduated, the original Nine had been reduced to seven. Their number now dwindled to five. In September 1958 Terrance Roberts headed to Los Angeles, California, to live with relatives while completing his senior year. Gloria's mother, Mary Ray, was forced out of her job due to her daughter's involvement with school integration, so Gloria also moved away from Little Rock. Daisy Bates helped arrange for the remaining students—Carlotta Walls, Jefferson Thomas, Elizabeth Eckford, Melba Pattillo, and Thelma Mothershed—to take courses offered by the University of Arkansas to high school students through the mail.

Orval Faubus's pro-segregation stand was popular with white voters. In November 1958 he became only the second governor in his state's history to win a third straight term. Furthermore, his tactic of blaming the school crisis on Daisy Bates also worked.

One afternoon in September 1958 Mrs. Bates was driving home from the *State Press* office when a car smacked into her rear bumper. Looking in her rearview mirror, she saw three teenage boys in the car that had struck her. One of them leaned his head out the window and threatened, "Get out of our way!"

Trying to avoid trouble, Daisy Bates drove on at her regular pace, but the boys tailgated her, swearing and shouting insults. She realized that she might have to defend herself, so she removed her pistol from the glove compartment and placed it on her lap. At a red light the car containing the hooligans pulled up alongside her. Suddenly, a youth jumped out of the backseat and ran up to Daisy Bates's open car window.

"You and those damn coons closed our school!" he yelled. As Mrs. Bates stared at him icily, he grabbed the handle of her door and said, "I ought to pull you out of that car and beat you to a pulp!"

Daisy Bates was about to flash her gun when one of the other boys grabbed the youth by his jacket and said, "Come on, we'll get her later!"

Two days later a firebomb was thrown at the Bates home from a speeding car. It landed in the driveway but burned out without doing any damage.

"They want to go slow, child. That's what they said 80 years ago."

Cartoon criticizing the slow pace of school integration.

There were numerous other incidents. Vearlon Jeffries is now a fifty-year-old mother of one son. In 1958 she was a four-year-old child growing up in the same home where she lives today—directly across from the Bates house on West 28 Street. Some of her earliest memories are of violence directed at Daisy and L.C. Bates.

"I remember things being constantly thrown at her house, including bricks through her window," Ms. Jeffries recalls. But the incident she remembers most vividly occurred one night in 1958. "My parents had told me to stay away from the living room window," because of all the dangerous things going on across the street, she said. "That evening I went to the window anyway. I was looking out the window, keeping my eyes glued to their house, when suddenly someone threw a firebomb on the Bateses' roof. I alerted my parents that Mrs. Bates's house was on fire." The fire department came and put out the flames before the blaze could spread.

Several months later there was another frightening incident. A car filled with white men sped down the street toward the Bates home. Suddenly, the men opened fire, spraying bullets around the neighborhood. The shots missed the Bates's house, but three bullets entered a room of a nearby home where small children were watching TV. Fortunately, nobody was hit.

The battle to reopen the high schools was waged on several fronts. The NAACP worked through the courts. Many members of Little Rock's business community also wanted to reopen the schools, for the educational crisis had given the city such a bad reputation that it couldn't attract any new major industries during the late 1950s. Also, during the 1957–58 school year, 1,500 white Little Rock women joined together as the Women's Emergency Committee to Open Our Schools (WEC).

Daisy Bates wanted to join the WEC, but its leaders thought the presence of black women would cause friction in the group. Adolphine Fletcher Terry, a WEC founder who once called Daisy Bates "the bravest woman I have ever known," warned her not to attend an organizational meeting. "Don't you come, Daisy, don't you come," Mrs. Terry insisted, "because if you do, I can't get the other women to come." Daisy Bates later wrote an article in which she reportedly criticized the WEC for "working *for* the Negroes, not *with* them." She never published it, however, because she felt that the WEC achieved a lot despite its flaws. The WEC helped elect a new school board that decided to reopen the high schools on an integrated basis in the fall of 1959.

The integration was minimal at first. Jefferson Thomas and Carlotta Walls were the only two of the original Nine left at Central. Also in the 1959–60 school year three black girls entered Hall High School, located in a well-to-do section of Little Rock. Once again there were demonstrations and fiery speeches by Governor Faubus at the start of the school year, but then things settled down. With the U.S. Supreme Court, the NAACP, and a growing number of white Little Rockians against them, the segregationists realized that their cause was lost.

Confident that school integration was on its way, Daisy Bates turned to other matters. By 1959 the bigots had nearly destroyed the *State Press*. The newspaper's circulation had plunged from a peak of 22,000 to just 6,000. Having faced

Daisy Bates receiving an award for her civil rights work.

bombs, fires, gunshots, and mobs to fight for what they believed in, L.C. and Daisy were especially disappointed that thousands of black readers had been intimidated into canceling their subscriptions. On the brighter side, now and then people who heard that the *State Press* was fighting for its life sent donations to help keep the newspaper afloat. One letter that touched Daisy Bates came from a Mississippi boy who sent her a fifty-cent piece along with a letter on notebook paper:

> Dear Miss Daisy,
>
>   I am ten years old and this is all I have. I was saving it to buy Mom a Christmas present. I want you to have it. I know she won't mind. I want to help.
>
> Larry

By the fall of 1959 the couple could no longer keep their newspaper going. On October 30, 1959—after eighteen and a half years—the *Arkansas State Press* released its final issue.

Daisy Bates was about forty-six and L.C. was fifty-eight years old when their newspaper died. He took its demise very hard, for as was later said at a testimonial in his honor, the *State Press* had been "his baby." His only consolation was that the newspaper had lasted long enough to help bring about school integration in Little Rock.

L.C. and Daisy Bates now had to find a way to earn a living. He took a position as a "troubleshooter" and field representative for the NAACP. The job mainly involved civil rights issues in Arkansas, but one assignment took him to Tennessee, where he worked on behalf of blacks who had been thrown off their farms because they attempted to register to vote. The NAACP considered the Tennessee mission so dangerous that they had L.C. phone national headquarters every few hours to reassure them that he was still alive.

Daisy Bates resigned as Arkansas NAACP president in 1959, after seven years at the helm. She then spent much of her time away from Little Rock on speaking tours and in New York City contacting publishers and writing her autobiography,

Mrs. Bates autographing copies of *The Long Shadow of Little Rock.*

The Long Shadow of Little Rock. Published in 1962, the book concentrated on her role in the Little Rock school crisis.

During the period in the early 1960s when L.C. was traveling for the NAACP and Daisy was off lecturing and promoting her book, the couple drifted apart. In February 1963 Daisy and L.C. Bates shocked many people by getting divorced. As with much of Daisy Bates's earlier life, the details of what happened remain hazy, and there are people who knew them well who to this day still don't believe they ever were divorced.

One possible reason for the divorce was that L.C. became jealous of his wife's fame. He had transformed her from an obscure country girl to an articulate and prominent woman. Now she was constantly away on speaking tours and hobnobbing with famous people, while he could no longer do what he liked best: run a newspaper. A person who knew both Daisy and L.C. Bates hinted at another possible cause for the divorce: At one point Daisy Bates apparently became infatuated with a newspaperman from New York and ran off with him for several weeks.

The divorce didn't last long, however. Still in love with each other, Daisy and L.C. remarried on July 12, 1963, just five months after their divorce. They remained married until separated by death seventeen years later.

"Things are looking up a little this year, sir."

February 12. 1959

This Bill Mauldin cartoon appeared on February 12, 1959, the 150th anniversary of Abraham Lincoln's birth; a child is telling Lincoln's statue that things are improving somewhat for the nation's African Americans.

16

The Power of One

The integration of Little Rock Central started a movement that spread all over the country. At the time, New York and Chicago schools were segregated, too. Now we've got black mayors in so many big cities. And it all started with the desegregation of a school.

Daisy Bates, 1984

Daisy Bates and the Little Rock Nine had paved the way for school integration to continue in Arkansas cities and towns. In Little Rock, however, change came slowly. By 1962 only eighty black children had been assigned to previously all-white junior and senior high schools in the Arkansas capital. Yet by the 1970s progress had been made in desegregating public schools throughout Arkansas and other parts of the country.

But the Little Rock Nine episode didn't just spark integration in America's schools. It awakened the nation's conscience to the evils of segregation and hatred. Millions of children who grew up witnessing the TV coverage and newspaper images of the Little Rock crisis later became active in the civil rights battles of the 1960s. The marches, freedom rides, sit-ins, and demonstrations they took part in led to legislation outlawing discrimination in jobs and housing. Hotels, restaurants, parks, and other public places were forced to desegregate as well.

The Little Rock school crisis shaped the lives of everyone involved. Governor Orval Faubus's anti-integration stand made him popular among many white voters. He served as Arkansas governor for twelve years (1955–67), the longest anyone had ever governed the state. But millions of people who followed events in Little Rock saw Faubus as the chief villain in a tragic chapter of American history.

During his later years Orval Faubus was often asked why he had blocked school integration. Not long before his death in 1994, Faubus told author Beth Roy that Arkansas citizens had elected him governor, and he had just attempted to do what most of them wanted. Moreover, he had tried to keep the black students out of Central High to prevent violence, Faubus insisted. Whatever his motives were, he lived long enough to realize that he would go down in history as a bigot. Historian Kermit L. Hall summarized Faubus's legacy when he wrote: "His actions appropriately made his name a byword for racism around the world."

One person's opinion must have especially stung the governor. During the crisis a man signing himself Jimmy Higgins wrote letters criticizing Governor Faubus that were published in the *Arkansas Gazette*. Jimmy Higgins was a false name used by the letter writer—Orval Faubus's own father.

The Ogden family had helped Mrs. Bates during the school crisis. On September 4, 1957, the Reverend Dunbar Ogden Jr., along with his twenty-one-year-old son, David, had been in the caravan of cars that had taken the black students to Central High. Reverend Ogden's congregation turned against him because of his support for integration, and some members stopped attending services. He was forced to resign and take a position as a minister in another state.

David Ogden, who remained in Little Rock, also became a target of the racists. One night outside a movie theater, a group of youths began calling David Ogden "nigger lover" and shouting, "Why aren't you with Daisy Bates?" At work, his colleagues called him a traitor to his race. One coworker punched him. David Ogden had to resign from one job after another. In June 1960 he was heading to California to look for work when, in a fit of depression, he killed himself while stopped at a motel.

Superintendent Virgil Blossom became one of the most disliked people in Little Rock. The racists loathed him for starting school integration, while others blasted him for not doing enough. Mr. Blossom received numerous threats from the bigots and once while driving was shot at by a sniper. Fortunately, the bullet missed him and struck his car door. In late 1958 Mr. Blossom was fired due to the school controversy. He later obtained a similar position in San Antonio, Texas.

Grace Lorch, who had tried to protect Elizabeth Eckford from the mob, was also despised by the racists. In early 1958 a bomb was found at the Lorch family's home. Apparently, it didn't go off.

No one endured more physical abuse during the school crisis than Alex Wilson, the Memphis *Tri-State Defender* editor who was beaten and struck in the head with a brick on September 23, 1957. Afterward he began to suffer headaches, and

Daisy Bates traveled a lot during the 1960s.

his health deteriorated. Diagnosed with the brain disorder Parkinson's disease, Wilson died in October 1960, three years after being attacked.

The parents and other relatives of the Little Rock Nine suffered in many ways. Ellis Thomas, Jefferson's father, was suddenly fired from his job with a farm machine manufacturer after more than ten years with the firm. Everyone knew he had lost his job because his son was one of the Little Rock Nine, but the company simply said his "services are no longer required." Gloria Ray's mother and Carlotta Walls's father were also forced out of their jobs because of their close connection to the Little Rock Nine.

If anyone doubted that they were serious about their educations, the Nine proved it after finishing high school. All of them went on to college, thanks partly to scholarship money Daisy Bates raised through the NAACP. Notes still exist in which Mrs. Bates calculated how much money each of the Nine would need for college.

Minnijean Brown attended the Mount Sinai School of Nursing in New York City and then Southern Illinois University. For a time she, her husband, and their six children lived and worked on a farm in Canada, but later Minnijean returned to live in Little Rock.

Elizabeth Eckford attended Knox University in Galesburg, Illinois, and later Central State College in Wilberforce, Ohio. When we interviewed her in 2003, Elizabeth was a probation officer living in Little Rock.

Ernest Green attended Michigan State University and later served as assistant labor secretary for employment and training under President Jimmy Carter. A Walt Disney movie, *The Ernest Green Story*, was made about Central High School's first black graduate.

Thelma Mothershed attended Southern Illinois University and in 1966 underwent surgery to repair her heart. She worked for many years as a teacher and school counselor in East St. Louis, Illinois, but in 2003 she told us she moved back to Arkansas because "I love Little Rock—that's my home."

Melba Pattillo attended Columbia University School of Journalism in New York City. She became a TV news reporter and wrote an acclaimed autobiography, *Warriors Don't Cry*.

Gloria Ray graduated from the Illinois Institute of Technology and became a prolific computer science writer. She married a man from Sweden and moved to that country.

Terrance Roberts attended the University of California at Los Angeles and earned his doctorate in psychology at Southern Illinois University. He is a professor of psychology at Antioch University in Los Angeles.

Jefferson Thomas graduated from Central High in 1960, then attended Wayne State University in Detroit. He later served in the Army and ran a record shop in the Los Angeles area.

Carlotta Walls also graduated from Central in 1960. She then attended Michigan State University. Carlotta lives in Denver, Colorado, where she sells real estate.

Because of the experiences they shared, the Nine have a special bond. "We think of ourselves as each other's best friends," Thelma Mothershed Wair said. With great feeling for her schoolmates, she added: "We are the Nine, first and last."

"We Nine are all tied together for life," Elizabeth Eckford told us, explaining that they still gather together periodically.

One of the last times the Nine met with Daisy Bates was at the fortieth anniversary of their entering Central High. Unlike 1957, when they often encountered curses, threats, and kicks at the school doors, the Nine were greeted at the 1997 reunion by President Bill Clinton, an Arkansas native who had served as governor of the state. Speaking from the steps of Central High School, President Clinton told the 7,500 people who had gathered for the celebration:

> *What happened here changed the course of our country forever. Like Independence Hall where we first embraced the idea that God created us all equal. Like Gettysburg, where Americans fought and died over whether we would remain one nation, moving closer to the true meaning of equality. Like them, Little Rock is historic ground. For, surely it was here at Central High that we took another giant step closer to the idea of America.*

MARCH ON WASHINGTON FOR JOBS AND FREEDOM
AUGUST 28, 1963

LINCOLN MEMORIAL PROGRAM

1.	The National Anthem	*Led by* Marian Anderson.
2.	Invocation	The Very Rev. Patrick O'Boyle, *Archbishop of Washington.*
3.	Opening Remarks	A. Philip Randolph, *Director March on Washington for Jobs and Freedom.*
4.	Remarks	Dr. Eugene Carson Blake, *Stated Clerk, United Presbyterian Church of the U.S.A.; Vice Chairman, Commission on Race Relations of the National Council of Churches of Christ in America.*

5.	Tribute to Negro Women Fighters for Freedom
	  Daisy Bates
	  Diane Nash Bevel
	  Mrs. Medgar Evers
	  Mrs. Herbert Lee
	  Rosa Parks
	  Gloria Richardson
		Mrs. Medgar Evers

6.	Remarks	John Lewis, *National Chairman, Student Nonviolent Coordinating Committee.*
7.	Remarks	Walter Reuther, *President, United Automobile, Aerospace and Agricultural Implement Workers of America, AFL-CIO; Chairman, Industrial Union Department, AFL-CIO.*
8.	Remarks	James Farmer, *National Director, Congress of Racial Equality.*
9.	Selection	Eva Jessye Choir
10.	Prayer	Rabbi Uri Miller, *President Synagogue Council of America.*
11.	Remarks	Whitney M. Young, Jr., *Executive Director, National Urban League.*
12.	Remarks	Mathew Ahmann, *Executive Director, National Catholic Conference for Interracial Justice.*
13.	Remarks	Roy Wilkins, *Executive Secretary, National Association for the Advancement of Colored People.*
14.	Selection	Miss Mahalia Jackson
15.	Remarks	Rabbi Joachim Prinz, *President American Jewish Congress.*
16.	Remarks	The Rev. Dr. Martin Luther King, Jr., *President, Southern Christian Leadership Conference.*
17.	The Pledge	A. Philip Randolph
18.	Benediction	Dr. Benjamin E. Mays, *President, Morehouse College.*

"WE SHALL OVERCOME"

Daisy Bates was one of the "Negro Women Fighters for Freedom" honored at the historic 1963 March on Washington.

L.C. Bates worked for the NAACP until the age of seventy. He spent much of his later life helping jobless people find work before retiring from the NAACP in January 1972. Five years later, as Mr. Bates approached his seventy-sixth birthday, 300 people from Little Rock and beyond honored him at a banquet. One speaker, Little Rock theater owner Lucille Babcock, said that L.C. had sacrificed "his baby, the *State Press,*" in the civil rights struggle. TV news reporter and Little Rock native Delois Handy declared that L.C. and Daisy Bates had helped "pave the way" for her and other blacks to enter fields previously denied them. Reflecting back on more than ten years of working under L.C. Bates at the *State Press,* type-setting machine operator Robert Scott said: "He practiced exactly what he preached. He helped those that needed help and fought for those things he knew were right."

Responding to the praise, L.C. said they shouldn't think the struggle was won. Plenty of work remained to be done before "some day, we may say not that we *shall* overcome, but that we *have* overcome."

During his last years L.C. suffered from two eye conditions, glaucoma and cataracts, and had trouble reading. Eventually, he lost his vision completely in his left eye. Yet up to his last day he nurtured a dream: He wanted to start another newspaper. He wasn't able to do this, for following surgery for an aneurysm (a bulge in a blood vessel), L.C. Bates died at St. Vincent's Infirmary in Little Rock on August 22, 1980, at the age of seventy-nine. Daisy and her goddaughter, Jan Brown, were at L.C.'s side at the end.

Daisy Bates had many more active years following her retirement as Arkansas NAACP president in 1959 and the publication of her autobiography three years later. Having become one of the nation's best-known black women, she served on the Board of Directors of the NAACP and also of the Southern Christian Leadership Conference (SCLC), which Dr. Martin Luther King Jr. had helped begin in 1957 to organize civil rights efforts in the South. On August 28, 1963, Mrs. Bates participated in the March on Washington, at which 200,000 people converged on the nation's capital. Dr. King made his famous "I Have a Dream" speech at this giant civil rights rally. Mrs. Bates was one of the civil rights leaders introduced to the huge crowd.

At the time of the March on Washington, black southerners were still generally excluded from voting and holding office. Federal civil rights legislation of the

1960s began to change this. After seeing firsthand how Governor Faubus and President Eisenhower had wielded their power in Arkansas, Daisy Bates realized that political involvement was a key to civil rights progress. In the early 1960s she spent a great deal of time in Washington, D.C., where President John F. Kennedy appointed her to the Democratic National Committee, and where she served as an adviser in President Lyndon B. Johnson's anti-poverty programs. But then in 1965 Mrs. Bates suffered her first stroke. She returned to Arkansas, where she lived almost all of her remaining life.

Following her recovery, she took up a new cause in one of Arkansas' poorest towns. Mitchellville was a mostly African American community located forty-five

Part of the crowd around the Reflecting Pool on the National Mall during the 1963 civil rights march on Washington, D.C.

miles from New Edinburg, where Daisy had once lived with her grandmother. In 1968 Mrs. Bates was named director of Mitchellville's Self-Help Project, a program that was part of President Johnson's War on Poverty. While in Mitchellville she lived in a mobile home, and she traveled regularly between the town and her home in Little Rock over several years. Among her achievements, she obtained new sewage and water systems, paved streets, and a community center for Mitchellville. When budget cuts threatened the Self-Help Project, she resigned and returned to Little Rock in 1974. Then sixty years old, Daisy Bates looked forward to a quiet retirement with L.C., who had recently left his NAACP job.

She did spend the next six years with L.C., helping to care for him as his health declined. After L.C.'s death in 1980, Daisy Bates made a surprising decision: She would fulfil her husband's dream and revive the *State Press*.

Friends and relatives doubted that she could do it, for L.C. had been the driving force behind the newspaper. Besides, a newspaper would require lots of money and energy. To make things even more difficult, Daisy Bates suffered another stroke around the time that L.C. died. David Neely, who had periodically visited his Bates cousins since his childhood, was in law school in the early 1980s. When he went to Arkansas following his cousin Daisy's stroke, he found her incapacitated in just one way. "She slurred her words," he recalled. "Most people couldn't understand what she was saying, but I could."

She told David that she hoped to restart the newspaper with him working at her side, much as David's mother, Lottie Brown Neely, had assisted L.C. forty years earlier in the pioneer days of the *State Press*. "She was always telling me I was a good writer, and that I reminded her of L.C.," David Neely told us. "Daisy Bates had a dream for me: that I would move to Little Rock and help her with the paper." At a time when black Arkansans were becoming more involved in the electoral process, Daisy Bates was also convinced that her young cousin David could have a bright future in state politics.

"She was a very influential figure in my life," said David Neely, thinking back about Daisy Bates's constant encouragement. However, he had his own plans for his future. "I was in my early twenties and in law school, and I didn't want to move to Little Rock." So instead of helping his cousin Daisy begin the newspaper, he completed law school and became a Chicago attorney.

That didn't stop Daisy Bates. She scraped together the money and in 1984 reopened the *State Press* with two partners, the Reverend Robert Willingham and school official Dr. H. Benjamin Williams. Mrs. Bates was seventy years old when the newspaper—of which she was two-thirds owner—sprang back to life. Regarding her reentry into the newspaper business as a senior citizen, Mrs. Bates explained in the September 1984 *Ebony* magazine: "I said to myself, *If you're going to do it, do it now or forget it.*"

The new *State Press* was similar to the old one—with articles of interest to African Americans and an emphasis on civil rights news. Her small staff, which helped her write, edit, and promote the newspaper, for a time included Ernest Green, who a quarter of a century earlier had become the first black graduate from Central High School. Mr. Green, who had served in President Jimmy Carter's administration as a specialist in employment and training, was the marketing director of the new *State Press.*

Daisy Bates also hired local youngsters to help distribute her paper. They included Courtney Peeples, whose mother, Vearlon Jeffries, had been the first person to notice that a firebomb had been thrown on the Bateses' roof more than twenty-five years earlier. "I used to pick up papers at the *State Press* and distribute them in the neighborhood around here," recalls Courtney. Now in his twenties, he was only about seven years old when he worked as a newsboy for Daisy Bates.

At first the new *State Press* attracted advertisers, explained David Neely. "Then something happened. A young black woman who lived outside Little Rock and who worked as a counselor for troubled youths was murdered. Three white guys lured her from her place of employment and raped and murdered her. Daisy was so outraged that she began following the trial and writing about it."

Businesses would stop advertising in the paper if she continued to focus on this racially charged murder, she was warned, much as had occurred years earlier during the school crisis. But, just as in 1957, she wouldn't be intimidated. Besides, she felt she had a personal stake in this case, for it reminded her of her own mother's murder seventy years earlier.

"Advertisers pulled out from the paper," David Neely continued. "She had to mortgage her house to finance the *State Press*." It was a losing battle, as she and L.C. had experienced with the demise of the original *State Press* nearly thirty years earlier. In 1987 seventy-four-year-old Daisy Bates sold the paper.

About the time that Daisy Bates retired from the newspaper business, she suffered yet another stroke. Her legs were affected, and afterward she needed a walker to get around. Her speech also worsened. "She had slurred her words before," explained David Neely. "Now it got to the point where she couldn't be understood. She'd get frustrated because her brain kept working and she had so much to say but she couldn't express it." Mrs. Bates found a solution: She com-

This 1991 portrait of Daisy Bates by Albert Smith hangs in the Arkansas State Capitol.

Eighty-two-year-old Daisy Bates carrying the Olympic torch in 1996.

municated by exchanging notes with David and other visitors, passing the messages back and forth across the table.

Daisy Bates was frequently honored in her last years. In 1984 the University of Arkansas awarded her an honorary Doctor of Laws degree. The Daisy Bates Elementary School in Little Rock was named for her in 1987. The following year a paperback version of *The Long Shadow of Little Rock* became the first reprint edition to win an American Book Award. In 1996 Daisy Bates, then eighty-two years old and in a wheelchair, carried the torch to help light the Olympic Flame for the Summer Games in Atlanta, Georgia. She was cheered on by friends, relatives, and admirers, some of whom cried at the sight of the civil rights worker bearing the Olympic torch in her wheelchair. Then, in 1997, Daisy Bates and the Little Rock Nine were honored at the fortieth-anniversary celebration at Central High by President Clinton.

But Mrs. Bates was suffering from something else besides the effects of her strokes. Due partly to the cost of reviving the newspaper, she was nearly penniless. In fact, she would have lost her house if not for the Christian Ministerial Alliance, a group of ministers who purchased her home so that she could continue to live in it.

Besides arranging for her to remain in her home, the Ministerial Alliance made sure she had food, medical care, and helpers around the house. Neighbors pitched in, too, including her young friend Courtney Peeples. "I'd drive her to the store, take out the trash, and do the dishes," recalls Courtney, who was about sixteen at the time. He would also help care for her eight cats, for in her old age Mrs. Bates rescued numerous cats from the Humane Society and brought them into her home.

"Despite her strokes she was still Mrs. Bates," Courtney continued. "She read all the time. She would sit at the table and read a book or the newspaper. Although she could walk a little, she mostly got around her house in her wheelchair."

The Reverend Leroy James, one of the people assigned by the Ministerial Alliance to monitor her welfare, visited Daisy Bates often during her last years. "She was mentally sharp till the end," says Reverend James. "In her last years she spent a lot of time watching TV, especially the news, for she never lost interest in

President Bill Clinton speaks to a crowd of 7,500 on the Central High School lawn on September 25, 1997, exactly forty years after the 101st Airborne troops escorted the Little Rock Nine to class.

Forty years later . . . Central High graduates.

what was happening in the world. And she always had books and magazines around."

She suffered another stroke in about 1998, and was nearly always in her wheelchair for the last year of her life. Daisy Bates died in Little Rock on November 4, 1999, at or very close to the age of eighty-six.

At a memorial service in her honor, President Bill Clinton told the audience: "What I'd like to say to you is that I really liked Daisy Bates. I liked her because she was a brave woman who fought the civil rights battle. But I liked her also because she was a brave woman who kept her spirits up."

After her death a street going past Central High School was renamed Daisy Bates Drive. Then in 2001 Arkansas became the first state to honor an African American woman with a state holiday. The third Monday in February is celebrated as the Daisy Bates Holiday in Arkansas. In preparation for this special day, schoolchildren are taught about Daisy Bates and how she led the fight for school integration in Little Rock half a century ago.

We asked a few people who knew her to express some final thoughts about Daisy Bates. Her goddaughter, Jan Brown, told us: "Because of how the Smiths loved her as a child, Daisy Bates had something in her spirit that directed her path to concern for children. She reached out to the Nine out of love and courage to let them know she would be a surrogate mother while they went through something

Today, the street running past Central High School is named for Daisy Bates.

that would be a turning point in the civil rights struggle—something that would help establish what the country is supposed to stand for—equality."

"She was a role model for youth—a motivator, an inspiration," said the Reverend Leroy James. "She showed the importance and power of one person. Individuals such as Daisy Bates can make a difference."

"I used to think that in Daisy Bates's time there was a massive movement she was part of," David Neely added. "She told me, 'Don't be fooled. A handful of organizers gets things going, then other people join in.' The same thing is true today." Back when he was young, David Neely also used to wonder what would happen when people like Daisy and L.C. Bates and Thurgood Marshall could no longer fight for civil rights. Now he knows the answer.

"Fighting for equality is like carrying the Olympic torch," he says. "We all have an obligation to pick up the torch and carry on, because people of all races are still suffering, still living in poverty, still denied an education, and still hungry, and we have to do something about it."

Daisy Bates couldn't have said it better.

Source Notes

Daisy Bates is abbreviated as DB.

The Daisy Bates Papers at the Wisconsin Historical Society in Madison are abbreviated as the DB Papers-WHS.

Daisy Bates's autobiography, *The Long Shadow of Little Rock,* is referred to as *Shadow of LR.*

Introduction: "The Bravest Woman I Have Ever Known"

p. xi Will Campbell calls DB "the beautiful and indomitable Daisy Bates" and compares her to Sojourner Truth on page xv of the introduction to Will Counts's book *A Life Is More Than a Moment.*

p. xii Elizabeth Huckaby's comment that "the devil himself" could not have been hated more by the segregationists than DB is on page 200 of Huckaby's book *Crisis at Central High.*

p. xii Adolphine Fletcher Terry's comments about DB's bravery and relationships with the Nine are quoted on page 56 of *Breaking the Silence* by Sara Alderman Murphy.

CHAPTER 1: "THE NEXT WILL BE DYNAMITE"
The information for this chapter comes from *Shadow of LR.*

CHAPTER 2: "Niggers Have to Wait"
Much of the information about DB's early life comes from *Shadow of LR* and from interviews with Beatrice Cowser Epps and Clifton Broughton.

p .7 L.C. Bates joked that his wife was thirty-five "give or take a couple years" in the November 3, 1957, *New York Post* article "A Woman Who Dared . . . Mrs. Daisy Bates" by Ted Poston.

p. 7 The "delayed birth certificate" comes from the DB Papers-WHS.

p. 8 Melinda Gatson Hunter's claim that Hezekiah Gatson was really DB's father is in the DB Papers-WHS.

p. 14 The information that Orlee Smith was a lumber grader comes from page 617 of the

May 1996 *Journal of Black Studies* article "Daisy Bates and the Little Rock School Crisis," by Carolyn Calloway-Thomas and Thurmon Garner.

CHAPTER 3: "Who Killed My Mother?"
The information for this chapter comes from interviews with Beatrice Cowser Epps and from *Shadow of LR.*

CHAPTER 4: "Hate Can Destroy You, Daisy"
Interviews with Beatrice Cowser Epps, along with *Shadow of LR,* provided much of the information for this chapter.
pp. 29–30   The information about L.C. Bates is from Irene Wassell's master's degree thesis *L.C. Bates: Editor.*
p. 31   The quote "You can give her a better life than she has down here" was provided by Lottie Brown Neely during a 2003 interview with the authors.

CHAPTER 5: Birth of the *Arkansas State Press*
Interviews with Clifton Broughton and Lottie Brown Neely provided the bulk of the information about DB in this chapter.
p. 36   The information regarding Little Rock in about 1940 is from *Redefining the Color Line* by John A. Kirk.
p. 38   Irene Wassell stated that DB and L.C. were married in Fordyce, Arkansas, on page 13 of *L.C. Bates: Editor.*
p. 39   "The Day We Hope For" appeared on the editorial page of the *Arkansas State Press.*

CHAPTER 6: "Do Something"
Shadow of LR and interviews with Lottie Brown Neely provided much of the material for this chapter.
pp. 43–44   The "City Patrolman Shoots Negro Soldier" article appeared on the front page of the *State Press* on March 27, 1942.
p. 49 Information about the Bateses' Arkansas Supreme Court case came from the DB Papers-WHS.

CHAPTER 7: "There Must Be Some Place in America"
Redefining the Color Line and *Shadow of LR* provided the information for this chapter.

CHAPTER 8: "You Will Refrain from Calling Me Daisy"
p. 57   DB's correspondence with Governor Francis Cherry is in the DB Papers-WHS.
p. 58   The summary of desegregation in the various states comes from pages 66–68 of *It Has Happened Here* by Virgil T. Blossom.
pp. 59–60   Information about Hoxie, Arkansas, comes from the DB Papers-WHS.
pp. 60–62   Information about the Blossom Plan and Blossom's encounters with L.C. and DB are chronicled in *It Has Happened Here*, pages 11–29.
pp. 62–63   The incident in which the attorney repeatedly called DB by her first name is described in Ted Poston's *New York Post* article "A Woman Who Dared . . . Mrs. Daisy Bates."
p. 63   The ruling by Federal Judge John E. Miller is described on pages 52–53 of *Shadow of LR*.

CHAPTER 9: "Daisy, Daisy, Did You Hear the News?"
pp. 65–66 Virgil Blossom describes the process by which he selected the students to integrate Central High on pages 19–21 of *It Has Happened Here*.
pp. 66–68   Information about the students selected to integrate Central High and their families comes from *Redefining the Color Line* and *Shadow of LR*.
p. 68   The incident in which Virgil Blossom tells NAACP leaders that the black students should model themselves after Jackie Robinson is described on page 107 of *Redefining the Color Line*.
pp. 69–70   The segregationists and their groups are described in *Redefining the Color Line* and *It Has Happened Here*.
pp. 72–73   The hearing before the Pulaski County judge, Murray O. Reed, is described on pages 60–61 of *It Has Happened Here*.
p. 73   The incident in which the racists drove past the Bates home honking and shouting is described on page 57 of *Shadow of LR*.
p. 74   The letter from Arkansas Attorney General Bruce Bennett is in the DB Papers-WHS.
p. 74   DB's conversation with Jefferson Thomas is recorded on pages 59–60 of *Shadow of LR*.

p. 75 L.C.'s quip about adding "some color to the occasion" is recounted in Ted Poston's November 1, 1957, *New York Post* article "7 Kids Who Tried."

p. 75 DB mentions Carlotta Walls accompanying her to Federal Judge Ronald Davies's courtroom to hear his decision on page 130 of *Shadow of LR.*

CHAPTER 10: "They're In!"

pp. 77–78 DB describes arranging to have a few ministers accompany the black students to Central High in *Shadow of LR,* pages 64–66.

p. 78 DB relates her phone calls to the police and the students on pages 65–66 of *Shadow of LR.*

pp. 78–79 The transcript of DB's telephone conversation with NAACP official Gloster Current is in the DB Papers-WHS.

pp. 79–81 Elizabeth Eckford's experience with the mob is described in *A Life Is More Than a Moment* on pages 33–39, and also in *Shadow of LR,* pages 69–71 and pages 73–76.

p. 81 The conversation between the Reverend Harry Bass and Lieutenant Colonel Marion Johnson was reported on page 1 of the September 4, 1957, *Arkansas Democrat.*

pp. 82–84 The clashes between President Eisenhower and Governor Faubus are chronicled in numerous issues of the *Arkansas Gazette* and *The Arkansas Democrat* in the fall of 1957.

p. 84 DB reveals Elizabeth Eckford's anger toward her on pages 71–72 of *Shadow of LR.*

pp. 84–86 The incident of the white woman trying to pressure DB into calling off school integration is described in *Shadow of LR,* pages 170–175.

pp. 86–87 A description of how the Nine finally entered the school is provided on pages 87–92 of *Shadow of LR.*

CHAPTER 11: "Some Victory!"

p. 89 DB describes how the policeman warned her to get away from the school on page 90 of *Shadow of LR.*

pp. 89–90 The Alex Wilson beating is described on pages 47–56 of *A Life Is More Than a Moment.*

pp. 90–91 The Thelma Mothershed near-fainting incident is described by Elizabeth Huckaby on pages 34–35 of *Crisis at Central High.*

p. 92 The attack on the *Life* magazine staff members is described on page 93 of *Shadow of LR.*

p. 93 The transcript of DB's conversation with Gloster Current is in the DB Papers-WHS.

pp. 93–95 President Eisenhower's television speech and the arrival of the federal troops are described in the *Arkansas Gazette* and *The Arkansas Democrat* of September 24 and 25, 1957.

p. 95 The comments the Nine made about the arrival of the federal troops are mentioned on page 104 of *Shadow of LR.*

p. 95 Melba Pattillo Beals's description of the soldiers is from pages 131–133 of her book, *Warriors Don't Cry.*

pp. 96–97 The conversation between Terrance Roberts, Thelma Mothershed, Minnijean Brown, and the reporters was described on page 1 of the September 25, 1957, *Arkansas Democrat.*

p. 97 DB described Ernest Green's pessimistic comments on page 106 of *Shadow of LR.*

CHAPTER 12: "See You Later, Integrator!"
Personal interviews, newspapers, and the DB Papers-WHS provided the bulk of the material for this chapter.

p. 99 Elizabeth Eckford's and Thelma Mothershed Wair's comments were made during interviews with the authors in 2003.

p. 100 Virgil Blossom reveals that several congressmen called to complain about the U.S. troops on page 122 of *It Has Happened Here.*

p. 100 The September 27, 1957, *Arkansas Gazette* reported Governor Faubus's "occupied territory" speech.

pp. 100–101 Melba Pattillo Beals repeatedly describes how the racists tormented the Nine in *Warriors Don't Cry.*

p. 102 Virgil Blossom writes that four white students were expelled from Central for tormenting the black students during the 1957–58 school year on page 174 of *It Has Happened Here.*

p. 102 DB's October 3, 1957, conversation with NAACP officials is in the DB Papers-WHS.

pp. 102–106 The letters to DB from around the world come from the DB Papers-WHS.

pp. 106–108 The panel discussion between the black and white students is reported in the October 20, 1957, *New York Times*.

p. 108 The October 3, 1957, *Arkansas Gazette* reported that a white girl who wished to remain anonymous saw an Arkansas National Guardsman ignore the attack on Jefferson Thomas and Terrance Roberts, and that a white attacker wanted to make life for the black students so "miserable" they would withdraw from school.

pp. 108–109 Elizabeth Eckford and Thelma Mothershed Wair recalled their mistreatment during interviews with the authors in 2003.

p. 109 Elizabeth Huckaby describes the "stare days" and "black days" on page 120 of *Crisis at Central High* and the lipstick messages on page 64 of that book.

p. 109 The racist cards are described on page 140 of *It Has Happened Here*, and pictured on pages 156 and 157 of *Crisis at Central High*.

pp. 111–113 The attack on Jefferson Thomas and DB's meeting with Virgil Blossom are described on pages 125–127 of *Shadow of LR*.

p. 113 During a 2003 interview, Elizabeth Eckford told the authors that people "turned their backs" on the problems.

CHAPTER 13: "Follow in Your Footsteps"

p. 115 DB describes her arrest and trial on pages 107–110 of *Shadow of LR*.

p. 115 The flyer showing DB's mug shot and rap sheet is in the DB Papers-WHS.

p. 116 The violence at the Bates home was reported in several newspapers.

p. 116 DB's quote about people who "wanted us dead" comes from page 111 of *Shadow of LR*.

p. 117 David E. Neely's recollections of life in DB's home come from his interview with the authors in 2003.

pp. 118–119 The telephone conversation between the black students and Jackie Robinson comes from a transcript in the DB Papers-WHS.

p. 121 Thelma Mothershed Wair mentioned the "lonely existence" of the Nine in her interview with the authors in 2003.

p. 121 Melba Pattillo Beals describes how she felt almost invisible on pages 208–209 of *Warriors Don't Cry*.

p. 121 Melba's comments about Minnijean wanting to win over her classmates with her singing come from page 193 of *Warriors Don't Cry.*

p. 122 There are references to the "White Christmas" episode on page 111 of *Crisis at Central High* and on page 146 of *It Has Happened Here.*

pp. 122–123 The Minnijean Brown chili-dumping incident is described on page 117 of *Shadow of LR,* pages 218–220 of *Warriors Don't Cry,* and pages 103–104 of *Crisis at Central High.*

pp. 124–125 Minnijean's name-calling exchange with the white girl and her expulsion from Central High are described on pages 119–120 of *Shadow of LR.*

p. 125 Elizabeth Huckaby admits that Minnijean's expulsion was unfair on pages 151–152 of *Crisis at Central High.*

p. 125 Minnijean's "half a friend" quote appears on page 159 of *Crisis at Central High.*

CHAPTER 14: "We Made It"

p. 127 The story about the grocer comes from page 176 of *Shadow of LR.*

p. 127 The information about the drop in *State Press* circulation comes from page 128 of *Redefining the Color Line.*

p. 127 The cancellation of the Bateses' household insurance is mentioned on page 52 of *L.C. Bates: Editor.*

p. 128 Terrance Roberts's momentary decision to withdraw from Central High is described on page 138 of *Shadow of LR.*

p. 128 The Valentine's Day attack is mentioned on page 243 of *Warriors Don't Cry.*

pp. 128–130 The Gloria Ray water-pistol episode is described on pages 142–145 of *Shadow of LR.*

p. 130 Ernest Green's conversation with DB about graduation is mentioned on page 147 of *Shadow of LR.*

p. 131 Melba's prayer for Ernest is on page 304 of *Warriors Don't Cry.*

p. 131 Dr. King's presence at Ernest Green's graduation is mentioned on page 217 of *Crisis at Central High.*

p. 133 Melba Pattillo Beals describes what Ernest Green's graduation meant to her and her family on page 304 of *Warriors Don't Cry.*

CHAPTER 15: "To Rid Our Nation of the Evils of Segregation"

p. 135 The tour of DB and the Little Rock Nine is described on pages 136–137 of *Shadow of LR.*

p. 135 Elizabeth Eckford described what a "relief" the tour was in her 2003 interview with the authors.

pp. 135–136 Melba Pattillo Beals relates that the Nine were considered heroes and heroines "up North" on page 306 of *Warriors Don't Cry.*

p. 137 The text of DB's speech on accepting the Spingarn Medal comes from the DB Papers-WHS.

p. 138 The six new laws granting Governor Faubus power to combat integration are described on pages 181–183 of *It Has Happened Here.*

p. 138 Governor Faubus's comment about DB finding "an honest job" comes from page 155 of *Shadow of LR.*

p. 138 The information regarding the 1,000 high school pupils who left school permanently during the 1958–59 school year is from page 90 of *Breaking the Silence.*

p. 139 The incident in which the teenage boys rammed into her car is described by DB on pages 158–159 of *Shadow of LR.*

p. 140 Vearlon Jeffries spoke to the authors about the firebomb at the Bates house during a 2003 interview.

p. 140 The incident of the gunshots directed at the Bates house is related in the DB Papers-WHS.

pp. 140–141 The struggle of the Women's Emergency Committee to Open Our Schools is the subject of *Breaking the Silence.*

p. 142 The letter from the Mississippi child named Larry is quoted on page 177 of *Shadow of LR.*

p. 142 The death of the *Arkansas State Press* is described on pages 66–69 of *L.C. Bates: Editor.*

p. 142 L.C.'s experiences as an NAACP worker are described on pages 71–72 of *L.C. Bates: Editor.*

p. 143 DB's and L.C.'s divorce and remarriage are chronicled on page 13 of *L.C. Bates: Editor* and on pages 159–160 of *Redefining the Color Line.*

CHAPTER 16: The Power of One

p. 145 DB's quote about the movement that the desegregation of Central High inspired comes from page 94 of the September 1984 *Ebony* magazine article "Whatever Happened to . . . Daisy Bates?"

p. 146 Orval Faubus's comments that he had just tried to do what most Arkansas people wanted appear on page 93 of *Bitters in the Honey* by Beth Roy.

p. 146 Kermit L. Hall's comments appear in his chapter "The Constitutional Lessons of the Little Rock Crisis" on page 131 of *Understanding the Little Rock Crisis,* edited by Elizabeth Jacoway and C. Fred Williams.

p. 146 The newspaper letters criticizing Faubus written by his own father are mentioned on page 106 of *Bitters in the Honey* and on page 40 of *Breaking the Silence.*

p. 146 The Ogden family's troubles are chronicled on pages 191–195 of *Shadow of LR.*

p. 147 Virgil Blossom describes the sniper attack on page 150 and his getting fired on pages 194–195 of *It Has Happened Here.*

pp. 147–148 Alex Wilson's health problems subsequent to his beating are described on page 47 of *A Life Is More Than a Moment.*

pp. 148–149 Information about what became of the Little Rock Nine comes from pages 217–218 of *Shadow of LR,* pages 221–222 of *Crisis at Central High,* and interviews with several of the Nine.

p. 149 The comments about what the Nine still mean to one another come from interviews with Thelma Mothershed Wair and Elizabeth Eckford in 2003.

pp. 150–151 L.C. Bates's later life and death are described on pages 72–77 of *L.C. Bates: Editor.*

pp. 151–157 Much of the information about DB's last years comes from interviews the authors conducted in 2003 with David E. Neely, Courtney Peeples, the Reverend Leroy James, and Jan Brown.

p. 154 DB's quote about restarting the newspaper comes from page 94 of the *Ebony* article "Whatever Happened to . . . Daisy Bates?"

Bibliography

Collection of Documents

Daisy Bates Papers, Wisconsin Historical Society, Madison, Wisconsin.

Books

Bates, Daisy. *The Long Shadow of Little Rock: A Memoir.* Fayetteville, Ark.: University of Arkansas Press, 1987 (reprint of 1962 edition).

Beals, Melba Pattillo. *Warriors Don't Cry.* New York: Pocket Books, 1994.

Blossom, Virgil T. *It Has Happened Here.* New York: Harper, 1959.

Counts, Will. *A Life Is More Than a Moment: The Desegregation of Little Rock's Central High.* Bloomington, Ind.: Indiana University Press, 1999.

Fiftieth Anniversary 1904–1954: Huttig Mill. Shreveport, La: Olin Mathieson, 1954.

Huckaby, Elizabeth. *Crisis at Central High: Little Rock, 1957–58.* Baton Rouge, La.: Louisiana State University Press, 1980.

Jacoway, Elizabeth, and C. Fred Williams, eds. *Understanding the Little Rock Crisis: An Exercise in Remembrance and Reconciliation.* Fayetteville, Ark.: University of Arkansas Press, 1999.

Kirk, John A. *Redefining the Color Line: Black Activism in Little Rock, Arkansas, 1940–1970.* Gainesville, Fla.: University Press of Florida, 2002.

Murphy, Sara Alderman. *Breaking the Silence: Little Rock's Women's Emergency Committee to Open Our Schools, 1958–1963.* Fayetteville, Ark.: University of Arkansas Press, 1997.

Roy, Beth. *Bitters in the Honey: Tales of Hope and Disappointment across Divides of Race and Time.* Fayetteville, Ark.: University of Arkansas Press, 1999.

Sterling, Dorothy. *Black Foremothers: Three Lives.* 2nd ed. New York: Feminist Press, 1988.

Master's Degree Thesis

Wassell, Irene. *L.C. Bates: Editor of the* Arkansas State Press. University of Arkansas at Little Rock, 1983.

Articles

Calloway-Thomas, Carolyn, and Thurmon Garner. "Daisy Bates and the Little Rock School Crisis: Forging the Way." *Journal of Black Studies,* May 1996, pages 616–628.

"Light in a Dark Corner." *American Lumberman,* January 28, 1905, pages 51–82.

"Whatever Happened to . . . Daisy Bates?" *Ebony,* September 1984, pages 92–94.

Bibliography

Newspapers

Afro-American, Baltimore, Maryland
Arkansas Democrat
Arkansas Gazette
Arkansas State Press
Chicago Defender
New York Post
New York Times
St. Louis Argus

Videos

Blackside, Inc., producers. *Fighting Back, 1957–1962* (part 2 of six part series *Eyes on the Prize: America's Civil Rights Years, 1954–1965).* Alexandria, Va: PBS Video, 1986.
Disney Educational Productions. *The Ernest Green Story*, 1993.

Interviews by the Authors

(All took place in 2003)
In Huttig, Arkansas:
    Louis Boyette
    Clifton Broughton
    Laura Manning
    Jovon Smith
In Little Rock, Arkansas:
    Jan Brown
    Elizabeth Eckford
    Reverend Leroy James
    Vearlon Jeffries
    Aaron Lovelace
    Laura A. Miller
    Courtney Peeples
    David Ware
In the Chicago area:
    Beatrice Cowser Epps
    David E. Neely
    Lottie Brown Neely
    Thelma Mothershed Wair

Picture Credits

The photographs in this book are from the following sources and are used by permission and through the courtesy of the copyright owners:

AP/Wide World: pp. 75, 98, 156
American Lumberman: pp. 9, 10, 21
Baltimore Afro-American: pp. 86, 112
From the collection of Bob Besom: p. 6
Butler Center, Central Arkansas Library System: p. 37
Central High Museum and Visitor Center: p. 94
Chicago Defender: pp. x, 24, 50, 71, 96, 129, 136, 141, 143, 147
Will Counts, from *A Life Is More Than a Moment*: pp. 72, 78, 80, 90, 91, 107, 124, 132, 157, 158
Denver Public Library, Western History Collection, Harry M. Rhoads, Rh-5940: p. 83
Judith Bloom Fradin: pp. xiv, 16, 56, 157, and Little Rock street signs on chapter-opening pages
Janis F. Kearney: pp. 44, 82, 116
Library of Congress: pp. 15, 32, 34, 40, 46, 52, 59, 64, 88, 101, 126, 136, 150, 152
Bill Mauldin Estate, copyrights by Bill Mauldin, reprinted by permission: pp. 55, 110, 139, 144
National Portrait Gallery: p. 118
State of Arkansas, Secretary of State: p. 155
Wisconsin State Historical Society: pp. 103, 116, 120
Wisconsin State Historical Society; photographed by Judith Bloom Fradin: p. 4

Index

Note: Page numbers in **bold** type refer to illustrations.

176